Latte Dreams

My one shot at coffee shop ownership

Steve Williamson

Dedicated to the memory of my dear brother, David Williamson, who gave so much to help others and embraced every opportunity to live a life of happiness and kindness. Rest in Peace. 1971–2022

TABLE OF CONTENTS

EPIGRAPH

It's November 2021, and I have just bought a coffee shop. I have never run my own business before, and nor do I have any experience of working in hospitality.

INTRODUCTION

I t's March, 2021. We have adjusted to a COVID-19 pandemic lifestyle. Many coffee shops, having been closed for the darkest months of the pandemic, have reopened and are as popular as ever (albeit with reduced seating). It's 10 a.m. and time for my morning brew. I escape from my home office and prepare myself a latte using my newly acquired 'Home Barista' espresso machine while having a kitchen conversation with Sheila, who is a good friend of my wife, Sharon.

"Are you still thinking about opening your own coffee shop?" Sheila asks.

"I'm still in love with the idea, but it looks like a tough business and part of me worries it will be the road to rack and ruin."

"Well, you've often said you get bored easily. Perhaps you just need a new project to focus on. And there's no denying you love your coffee. You make quite a fuss with your coffee beans and that hi-tech espresso machine you've just bought; anyone would think it was your life support. Is it any good?"

"It's more complicated than it needs to be to tell you the truth, especially with all those grind settings and its water filter. The instruction manual is excessively detailed, and I haven't quite mastered how to do milk texturing, or whatever the correct technical term is. I guess it's been designed for obsessive coffee connoisseurs."

"It looks like an expensive piece of kit."

"Probably equivalent to a full year's spend at Starbucks." I sip my over-frothed latte from a tall ceramic coffee cup, "but I do love a freshly brewed coffee to start the day."

"Well, you're not the only one who likes good coffee. In town, there are three coffee shops within one hundred yards of each other. They always seem to be busy, especially at lunchtime. Someone's making good money from them."

And with that comment, the die is cast. I have time on my hands, savings in the bank and Sheila has just pulled the trigger.

Within five days I've read two books on how to start up a coffee shop and started a commercial property search.

There is one slight nuance to this impending business venture. I already have a full-time job – one to which I remain committed. I work for a life sciences company, dealing with cyber security. My official place of work is our head office in London, but I am now functioning as a 'hybrid worker' from my home in the East Midlands town of Kettering, ninety miles due north of London. This arrangement has given me work-time flexibility, and so long as I continue to attend the necessary meetings and deliver on my objectives, there is no big push for a return to pre-pandemic work normality. It also affords me the opportunity for a side gig, such as coffee shop ownership, but I will need someone to manage it day-to-day. I contact my son, Kieran, who lives fifty miles away in Birmingham, and ask him if he would like to go into partnership and manage a coffee shop for me. He works in hospitality already and loves the idea of managing a coffee shop. One week on from that kitchen conversation and my vague semi-retirement dream is crystallising into a feasible prospect.

Kieran is twenty-four years old and works in a quick-service Asian restaurant in Birmingham city centre; he is a supervisor, with experience in both front-of-house and back-of-house, and so he should be able to step up to become a manager. I'll take care of the business side of things and Sharon will deal with staffing and community outreach such as art clubs and 'knit and natter' events. Together, we are adventurers, embarking on a business journey; Sharon is racing ahead and is already talking to people about 'our caff.'

Kieran is the one with the most relevant experience. Sharon has run her own business in the past, but that was a high-street optician. I have a beyond-tenuous link to the hospitality industry from a Saturday job I had forty years ago, which involved selling pies and Bovril at a low-capacity Scottish football ground. But using that as a measure of competence is a bit like claiming my tadpole-fishing escapades in a village pond qualify me as a North Sea trawlerman. I am humble enough to recognise our steep learning curve, and fortunately, we have people who can help us, such as Zoe – another friend. She is an accountant who has supported other people in business start-ups and is willing to help us with all things financial. With these collective skills and the wind in our sails, I think we make a great team.

So why have I decided on this? After all, there are easier ways to invest one's savings.

Firstly, I love coffee. Indeed, I've reached that stage in life where a freshly prepared latte has become a daily necessity. Without it, my family, friends and colleagues would have to endure my cantankerous mood for most of the day. That double-shot of espresso is my slow-release happy pill, and where better to indulge than in my own coffee shop?

Secondly, I love the coffee shop culture. In the great sphere of hospitality, the humble coffee shop serves a unique purpose as a social hub, where we catch up with friends or colleagues and pontificate over topics as diverse as the pitiful performance of the national football team or the latest railway strike. The coffee shop also offers what I refer to as social solitude: in other words, an alternative habitat for individuals who would otherwise be alone in their home (such as home workers) or those who simply find contentment in their proximity to others – where they can read or browse their smartphone or just watch the world go by.

The third and most important reason is business. I have been a contributor to the Starbucks revenue stream for many years. They have friendly staff and serve an adequate cup of coffee, but owning my own coffee shop is something I've had in the back of my mind as a vague semi-retirement plan for some time and one which should generate additional income.

This isn't just a sentimental post-pandemic project, it's also an investment opportunity that will consume most of my life savings, so it must generate a return on investment.

My initial research, using industry sources such as the World Coffee Portal, confirms my assumption that the coffee shop business is one of continued growth. There are over ten thousand branded coffee shop outlets in the UK, and this number continues to grow, fuelled, in part, by challenger brands such as Black Sheep and Esquire entering the marketplace. Interestingly, despite the increased concentration of premium coffee shops in town centres, there is no evidence of pricing wars. In fact, the cost of a 12-ounce latte has increased by 20% in recent years. This is an important insight, which indicates that consumers choose quality over price when it comes to their daily ritual.

This beckoning business opportunity seems too good to be true and one wonders why more entrepreneurs aren't taking a shot at this marketplace. Shopping centres and high streets still seem to be dominated by the big brands such as Costa and Starbucks; I suspect that any attempt to replicate their operating model would be a fool's errand, as an independent would never achieve the same economies of scale or have the resources to match their marketing muscle. However, in an ocean of whales there must be opportunities for the small fish to thrive, and this is where I see myself fitting in – as an independent operator carving out a niche in this rich ecosystem.

Our first major decision is to choose a start-up strategy. There are three ways to enter the coffee-shop business:

- Buy into a franchise
- Greenfield start-up
- Acquire an existing business.

Costa Coffee operate under a franchise model, whereby business investors buy a store and operate it using their proven (and profitable) business system, which covers everything from menu development to staff training. But a franchise comes at a high cost – I saw one listed on a business forum with an £800,000 price tag. That's a big investment for the privilege of being tethered to someone else's product range. A greenfield start-up approach means finding premises, fitting them out, and building up the business from scratch. This is likely to be the least expensive means to get started, but also the most time-consuming due to the need to establish operating procedures, recruit and train staff and negotiate with suppliers. Many of these greenfield start-ups close within the first year, either due to poor financial management or low footfall. Also, building a loyal customer base from nothing would mean a longer lead time to profitability. Acquiring an existing coffee shop has many advantages, not least an established customer base and trained staff. This would be a ready-made business, which would allow us to walk in and start operating with minimal effort. There would also be a trading history, which we could use to assess the true value of the business. However, under UK TUPE law, we would have to retain all existing employees. A change of ownership can be unsettling for staff; they may not even like us, and their preferred ways of working may not fit with our vision for the business, leading to conflicts and inefficiencies.

A franchise seems like the safe option, but the prospect of borrowing so much money is about as palatable as a sour-milk mocha. A greenfield approach carries the greatest uncertainty, but it is best for building our own unique brand identity, which is attractive as we are keen to go all-in for speciality drinks and eco-friendliness. Acquiring an existing business could be the easiest option, but successful ones normally come at a price premium. However, we are still in a post-pandemic business recovery phase, which means there could be some distressed coffee shops on the market which are priced for a quick sale.

I pause to consider the journey we are about to embark on, in the same way a skydiver may pause before jumping out of an aircraft at ten thousand feet. This venture would risk most of our personal savings for the thrill of business ownership. If successful, we would have a supplementary income and may even expand.

If we fail, we pick ourselves up, lick our wounds and get on with our working lives.

PART 1

THE STEAM STATION

I drive to Birmingham and pick up Kieran outside his rented flat. We are both dressed in business attire. I'm wearing a blazer with a pocket handkerchief; I've ironed a shirt and polished my shoes. Kieran has his hair slicked back and is wearing a black cashmere overcoat. We are pursuing a greenfield start-up strategy as our motivation is to build our own identity and create a unique menu which will differentiate ourselves from the competition. We have an appointment to view a small commercial premises in a suburb of Birmingham, which has come on the market. Until recently it was a Greggs store and is now vacant and available for a rent of £10,000 a year – within our budget. It is situated in a thoroughfare with retail outlets such as a travel agent, a pharmacy, estate agents, a speciality cake shop, and a WH Smith. The footfall seems to be made up of shoppers and office workers. We park in the Sainsbury's car park, which is directly across the road.

The agent has arranged an open viewing, and we arrive, as instructed, at 11 a.m., along with approximately twelve other interested parties. It's not as large as we would like; I estimate the customer zone would seat sixteen people at a squeeze, but I can see strong potential for takeaway trade. It has floor-to-ceiling windows and a large pavement area, ideal for outside seating. In the back shop, Kieran mentally itemises the kitchen equipment and points to the manager's office, which looks more like a converted broom cupboard with a small computer desk and chair. The agent is standing by the front entrance, iPad in his hand, having brief exchanges with the other viewers. I manage to get his attention and say we are very interested and ask if he could tell us what sort of tenant the landlord is looking for. He shrugs his shoulders and says, "Someone with the wherewithal to take on a ten-year lease." I interpret that as meaning someone with a track record in business and financial security.

Next day, I contact the agent to talk about putting in an offer, and I need to provide background information such as trading history of our company and date of incorporation. We have one day to submit our offer as other parties are doing likewise. I'm beginning to realise that we are disadvantaged when it comes to finding suitable premises. Retail units in locations with high foot traffic are much sought after, and commercial landlords prefer the security of established businesses which have the resources to commit to a long-term lease. We didn't even get on the shortlist for the vacant Greggs premises.

Our search continues. A couple of vacant cafes catch the eye: one was once a wizard-themed tea shop in a south Birmingham residential area; the other a former pub that had been converted into a coffee shop and has since closed. Closer inspection reveals they are situated in low-footfall zones, and that most likely explains their current dormancy.

One week later, we discover a hidden gem in the suburbs of Birmingham. It's a mile or so from the Bournville Village, the home of Cadbury World. The shop unit is vacant. It had been operating as a discount shoe shop but became another victim of lockdown-induced business extinction. The unit is positioned in a small shopping layby that cuts off the main arterial road into the city and is nestled between a tattoo parlour and a hairdresser. Less than fifty metres away is the front entrance to Kings Norton Train Station. There is one other coffee shop in the area, approximately quarter of a mile away, and to get there involves crossing a main road.

We meet the agent outside the shop. He's young, suited up, wearing a large-knotted necktie and is holding a thick hardback notebook. In our earlier phone conversation, he described it as a great location unit, which would benefit from some modernisation. He unpadlocks the metal shutters, rolls them up and we all go inside. The flooring is threadbare carpet with a strip of gaffer tape running across the middle of the floor to hide the joins. Fluorescent tube lighting is suspended from the ceiling. I give it a quick scan and estimate we could have seating for at least thirty people there. A flimsy floor-to-ceiling hardboard partition towards the rear separates the kitchen/toilet area from the rest of the shop. We wander in. This area has a concrete floor, some exposed electrical wiring from one of the walls and crumbling plaster reveals brickwork. There is a large, frosted window with vertical metal bars, presumably for enhanced security. We are pleased to see a single toilet cubicle, although the porcelain bowl is cracked, and I wouldn't feel safe sitting under that overhead pull chain cistern. This place is a long way off health and safety standards.

"Is the landlord going to do any repairs?" I point to the front window that has a large crack in it. "It's going to need more than a lick of paint before we can start serving food," I say.

"The landlord says he's prepared to offer a six-month rent-free period, to allow you to do repairs and fit it out. Then the rent will revert to ten thousand a year on a ten-year lease," he says.

Sharon, Kieran and I huddle together for a quick conflab and unanimously agree that this place is ideal. It gives us the blank canvas we are looking for – a perfect project for a skilled hand and a creative mind.

I start taking measurements and sketching out layouts. Sharon is more spatial and visualises how it should look.

"So, we should have the counter areas here," says Sharon. She is facing the side wall, arms outstretched. "Then, when customers come through the door, the first thing they see is the service counter. We'll have the pastry stand on one side and coffee machine on the other."

The agent is pointing towards the back of the shop. "That might not work there because remember the water supply comes from out back and the wastewater drains to the left-hand side of the shop," he says.

"That's for the plumber to sort out," says Sharon.

The agent nods his head, takes a few steps backwards, realising he has just been reprimanded.

"We can put some large pot plants in each corner." Sharon points to each of the front corners.

"That works," I say, and I draw two circles on my sketch. "I'm thinking of some tall bar stools positioned under a ledge in the front window. People can sit there with their laptops or hang out while waiting on their train."

Our viewing lasts over an hour. I suspect the agent missed his next appointment as he keeps looking at his watch and has made two phone calls. He doesn't object to our overstay as he can clearly see we are going to commit to this place. Perhaps he also wants to avoid another exchange with Sharon. We tell the agent we'll take it and ask for next steps.

"I'll draft the *Heads of Terms*, which outlines the intention to lease. If you can give me your solicitor's details, I'll send it to them. The landlord's solicitor will draft the contract and once agreed, it's signed and it's all yours," he says.

"How long will the whole process take?" I ask.

He takes a sharp intake of breath. "That depends on the solicitors. Possibly six weeks."

I look to Sharon and Kieran. "That will probably work out well as we need to get estimates for repairs and plumbing," I say.

It's 30th April, 2021. Over the last two weeks, I've prepared an outline project plan, obtained quotes from tradespeople and costed out equipment and furnishings. Our timeline for the refit and opening is two months from signing the contract, which means we should have a summertime opening. The biggest uncertainty is the legal process. We are currently waiting on the contract and lease to be drafted and for our lawyer to complete due diligence enquiries. It feels a bit like buying or selling a house where the necessary but frustrating legal process commences with an indeterminate timeline for its completion. On the plus side, this affords us time for detailed planning, such as interior colour schemes, menu development, visits to coffee roasters and general research. We also visit numerous coffee shops to take pictures of their menu boards and cake displays.

We have decided to name our soon to be establishment, *The Steam Station*. It is on theme as we are in the industrial heartland of the West Midlands and next door to a train station. Kieran has a marketing student friend with whom he is working on brand identity and various social media ideas. Sharon has contacted a local artists' club, who are enthusiastic about exhibiting in our shop once we open.

The proposed shop is fifty miles away from where Sharon and I live, but only six miles from Kieran's house. I'm finding this slightly problematic as it means most of our planning work is being conducted from home, but we make it work. Tradespeople get the keys from the agent and prepare their respective quotes. The biggest jobs are the plumbing (£4,300), electrics (£3,200) and air conditioning (£6,000). New flooring will be £2,500 if we lay it ourselves or double that if we get a professional to do it. I have put a handyman friend on standby for painting and joinery work.

Back home, the spare room is filling up with boxes of speciality teas and random merchandise, which Sharon gathers daily. I count over eighty boxes of tea – everything from Earl Grey to organic Genmaicha. Then there are drinking flasks, an eclectic mix of reusable cups, random trinkets and art materials.

"What do you think about selling these vacuum-insulated eco-cups?" Sharon thrusts one in front of me and obscures my eyeline to my laptop screen. "I spoke to the company today and they can put our own branding on them."

"You don't think we're getting out over our skis, do you? The spare room is filling up with clutter and we haven't even got the keys yet."

"Just getting organised," she says.

"I was reading through the Starbucks annual report the other day and there was a section on their retail mix – you know, the revenue split between beverages, food and merchandise. Stuff like reusable cups and general retail is less than 5% of their total sales. It's just incidental," I say.

"I thought you said we shouldn't try to imitate Starbucks."

"Yes, you're right, I did say that."

"I know I'm right. Also, I'm arranging a university reunion with my friends for some time next month. I thought we would host it at The Steam Station – it would be our first official function."

"Too soon." I point to my laptop screen and show her the colour-coded spreadsheet, with the red cells showing tasks that are overdue. "Best find a pub. We might not even have the keys by then. The solicitors are moving at a snail's pace."

"Do you want me to talk to them?"

"Good God, no!"

"What?"

"I mean, no need. I spoke to them yesterday. They're on the case and I'll keep on top of them," I say.

"Well, it's good to have a target to aim for. I'll tell my university friends we'll host it and if it's not ready, we'll just choose another venue."

The legal process drags on. The landlord's solicitor originally informed us that the draft lease will be ready for our review on the week of 13th May. It is now mid-June, we have just received the draft contract, and our solicitor has raised twenty-five enquiries against it; some of them are straightforward, such as requesting a copy of the asbestos report, others are more mysterious such as a reference to covenants originating from 17th February 1873 which prohibit the use of the property for commercial purposes. I can see we are making progress, but it feels like I'm riding a bike through a quagmire. I nag my solicitor to accelerate.

It is at this stage that I tell Kieran he should hand in his notice at his current job as we will need him hands-on and full-time as soon as possible. He has already worked out staffing levels and drafted job descriptions for the roles we need. I've created a website and a Facebook page, both of which are light on content other than a banner saying, 'Opening Soon.'

This protracted legal process has afforded me the time to learn more about running a coffee shop and preparing for business ownership. I've formed a limited company — Williamson's Coffee Shops Limited, registered with an accountant and commenced the process of opening a business bank account. I choose Lloyds as they have a branch close to our location and this will be useful for depositing cash and getting change. The online application is straightforward, then comes the red tape. I cannot open an account unless I can evidence my business premises, such as with a signed lease or a utility bill. I speak to someone at the bank, who is very good at explaining their account opening procedure, but at a loss to advise on what I could do to open the account ahead of my taking over the premises. I eventually reach someone who instructs me to ask my solicitor to write a letter confirming that I am about to become a tenant at the stated address. However, his initial letter is rejected because it doesn't contain the precise wording they require. They provide me with the specific wording (two sentences) they will accept. My solicitor rewrites the letter. It is accepted and I now need to wait approximately four weeks for my application to be processed and an account opened. There are times when I feel there is some supernatural force conspiring against our best efforts to start a small business.

I speak with potential suppliers, who, unlike the bank, appreciate the prospect of having us as customers. There is no shortage of roasters or equipment distributors, but one company I am attracted to is Jute Coffee. They are a small independent roaster who can provide a great start-up package, including coffee, syrups, equipment, training, support and recycling. They are a zero-waste business who convert used coffee grounds into coffee logs for burning, which fits very well with our own ethos. I spend an hour with the owner and come away feeling this is someone I trust and could do business with. As for an espresso machine, I've narrowed my choice down to either the Fracino Contempo or the Conti X-one Evo (made in Monaco). Both have three groups and two steam wands, which is a good specification to ensure thermal stability during high-usage periods. I also have the option of red colouring, which will look great on the countertop – a bit like having a sports car in the driveway.

The more I learn, the more my project plan expands, especially the budget, which is inflating like a red balloon in front of my eyes. Back in April, I had an aspirational start-up budget of £30,000. I now have a capital expenditure forecast of £65,000 – and that's after downgrading our furniture and planning to do even more of the refit ourselves.

It doesn't end there. We will also have to bank some working capital for initial stock and to see us through the first three months of trading – including paying salaries and utility bills. I take some comfort in the knowledge that the plan is realistic, but my anxiety levels are rising as I become increasingly conscious of our financial liability.

I decide to seek professional advice and engage the services of Andrew and Claire Bowen, coffee shop and café coaches. They have a strong background in running coffee shops and are authors of the book, *The Daily Grind, How to open and run a coffee shop that makes money*. Their perspective is pure business, with a heavy focus on the management disciplines necessary to run a profitable operation. We meet initially via Zoom. I have prepared a PowerPoint presentation, which includes cash flow forecasts, graphical illustration of the premises and sample menus. We start with introductions and pleasantries.

"So, why are you doing this, Steve?" asks Andrew. "What is your endgame?"

"It's a passion we have," I say. "It will also give my son Kieran an opportunity to manage his own place, and we want it to be profitable. So, I want to run this as a proper business. We're making good progress, but I don't know what I don't know – and that's why I'm talking to you."

"It's a pity you didn't get in touch sooner. It's normally best if we work with you right from the outset – before you've settled on a location," says Claire.

"Too late for that now," I say.

"Why don't you take us through your plans, Steve, and what your next steps are?" says Andrew.

I walk them through my corporate-style presentation and cover floor layouts, cash flow forecasts, staffing models, proposed menus and photographs of the location. I then display a Google Maps screenshot that shows its proximity to the train station and the arterial road into and out of the city.

Andrew is writing continuously as I talk.

"What's going to be your differentiator?" asks Claire.

"We want to be known as the place to go for great-tasting coffee. We also plan to do freshly baked cakes and pastries." I flip to our sample menus, which I have crafted using a graphics package – chalkboard style with rainbow-coloured chalk writing.

"And what margin are you achieving with these prices?" asks Andrew.

"We should make at least 50% on food, even more on coffee. I've checked the wholesale prices so I can be confident of that."

Andrew shakes his head. "You need to go for 75% margin and account for wastage."

"Who are your typical customers?" asks Claire.

"Commuters, shoppers, and local residents who want to hang out – or do some work there rather than at home."

"Have you seen our location checklist?" asked Andrew. "It's a good tool to assess footfall and the type of customers you're going to attract."

"Yes, I have seen that, but we live fifty miles away so haven't done a location survey. But we know it's a busy location and we should pick up customers coming and going to the train station."

They look at each other but make no comment.

"I'm hoping you can review our proposed internal layout." I skip to the 3D schematic, which shows the counter and seating layout, and I describe how we've selected furniture such as bench seating which will be positioned against the wall, as this maximises seating space.

"I like the floor-to-ceiling windows at the front," says Andrew, "that will be great for people watching. Customers like that."

"Why is your kitchen out the back and your serving counter near the front?" asks Claire. "It's a long way to walk to the counter." She points at the screen and waves her finger from one side to the other.

"Well, that's where most of the electrics are, and they have a separate sink there."

"I would put it alongside the counter, otherwise staff will use the kitchen to chat and hang out. You also need to think about speed of service," says Claire.

Other than kitchen positioning, they are impressed by my choice of furniture and layout, which makes best use of the space. I introduce the art theme and Sharon's idea to affix a wall-mounted chalkboard along one wall for customers to draw on.

"Art is good, but I wouldn't have the chalkboard," says Andrew. "I guarantee, within a week, someone will draw a knob and pair of bollocks on it."

This first meeting feels like a *Dragons' Den* experience – direct questions and blunt advice – which is exactly what I am looking for. We talk in detail about profit margins, as well as types of food items that are popular and would achieve the necessary margin. Importantly, they educate me on product pricing. We agree to continue our engagement, so we have a successful opening and get on the path to profitability.

My confidence is building once again as I progress with all necessary tasks, although my bank account application still seems to be stuck in a logjam. My project plan has fifty lines of tasks and a budget far more than what I originally anticipated. The forecast costs are now more than double my initial estimate:

Category	Cost estimate	Status
Admin, Legal, Consultancy & Insurance	£2,962	Limited company set up and trading name registered (The Steam Station)
Counter and Equipment	£27,000	Espresso machine, 2 grinders, oven, dishwasher, blenders, refrigerators and large freezer, food-prep equipment and counter furniture
Refurbishment, plumbing, electrical and aircon	£19,200	Based on best quotes received
Shop Furniture	£4,000	
Property Deposit	£3,000	
Initial stock	£2,000	
Additional working capital	£10,000	Staff salaries for two months
Total Estimated Cost	**£68,162**	
Actual spend so far	**£2,112**	

It has been over three months since we agreed to take on the coffee shop. The draft lease has now been reviewed, almost all the enquiries have been responded to, and the solicitor informs us that we will be able to sign the Tenancy Agreement next week. We make an appointment for the Wednesday and arrange to collect the keys at the same time. I've allowed two months for a complete refurbishment, booked an extended holiday from work and put tradespeople on standby. All going well, we should be open by the second half of September.

Our second attempt at developing a menu is dragging on. Kieran and I decide to dedicate a full Saturday to this task. I head up to his place in Birmingham early in the morning. He is a details person and is good at explaining the nuances of different side options for scones and toast.

"If a customer wants two slices of toast, that also means two butters and a small pot of jam, so the cost will be this –" he points to the spreadsheet cells – "so the selling price needs to be £1.80."

It is a painful process but an essential discipline for all hospitality business owners.

"We don't have any products over £5.00," I say. "I think we need to find some star products, Kieran, so we can push up the average transaction cost."

We browse the wholesaler's online store, looking for further inspiration, specifically food items that are easy to prepare, appealing to customers and yet at a price level that will give us the 75% profit margin we need.

It's lunchtime, and we drive to our soon-to-be coffee shop location to feed ourselves and perform some on-the-ground reconnaissance. Our first stop is the one other coffee shop in the area. It's one o'clock, and there are two other customers – one man working on a laptop and an older man looking at his phone. The decor is ageing, with peeling wallpaper and frayed carpets. The two members of staff flit between the back kitchen and counter; both look disinterested. We finish our lattes and leave to explore what else this locality has to offer (we should probably have done this long before now). Greggs takeaway has no customers. Next door but one is a Subway, which has one customer. There is a small Italian restaurant nearby, with inside and outside seating. It too is light on custom. We walk in the opposite direction, towards a residential area behind the block of shops where our coffee shop sits. We discover a footpath that leads directly on to the train station platform. This is convenient for residents. Unfortunately, it completely bypasses our coffee shop. The coffee shop is not even visible from the footpath and even if they knew about our place, it would involve a two-hundred-metre detour from the station platform just to buy our coffee.

Kieran continues to tell me about branding and social media marketing, but he can't see what I can see. We are back on the main road, outside our shop. I gaze up and down and see a few people standing at a bus stop. Other than that, there's hardly any footfall. Where else in the UK would you find an empty Greggs on a Saturday afternoon? For the first time, I start to wonder where our customers are going to come from.

It's early the next morning and I have not slept well. Sharon and I have a serious conversation. This is a large financial commitment and I feel that signing a ten-year lease in this location would be like a prison sentence. My location research, which was based on Google Maps and knowledge of a train station nearby, was flawed and created a delusion of heavy footfall.

I phone Kieran and have a conversation he was not expecting. He tries to convince me on the merits of the location and plays back everything I have been espousing for the last few months; but despite our visit the previous day, his perception hasn't shifted the way mine has. I tell him we will continue looking and this is just a setback, and we must make difficult decisions sometimes.

It's Monday morning. I'm contacting the solicitor and instructing them to pull out. We will not be coming into the office on Wednesday to sign the contract and we will not take on this lease under any circumstances. I could have told a convincing lie, such as "I've just lost my job" or "I've been diagnosed with a chronic illness," but I tell the truth and face up to the mistake. The money we have spent on solicitor's fees will go down as a sunk cost. Back home, we have a house full of product samples and merchandise that we will have to live with for a while longer. Of greater concern is the fact that I have just put my own son out of work.

A COFFEE SHOP TOWN

Our plan for refurbishing and opening The Steam Station was a meticulous one, covering everything from kitchen refit to coffee suppliers. But my failure to properly research the location meant the project was destined to create a perpetual loss-making white elephant. It's a bit like planning a military operation that brings us face to face with the enemy, before realising we don't have any weaponry. To think, we almost signed a ten-year lease on that one. We dodged that bullet and our mission continues – we must have a coffee shop.

As with all battles – military or business – a defeat is only a disaster if you don't learn from the experience. Fortunately, we are now much better informed on this industry and the key lesson to learn is the importance of location as coffee shops depend almost exclusively on passing footfall. A second realisation is the fact that securing suitable premises is not as easy as I thought it would be; or, to be more precise, finding a retail unit of a manageable size in a high-footfall location seems unattainable for a start-up like us.

We have changed our strategy. Rather than seek out a retail unit for refurbishment, we will search for an existing business to take over – one that has an active customer base and potential to grow. We are also widening our search radius.

Several potentials grab our attention: a small sandwich bar near an office complex; a coffee shop that doubles as a cocktail bar in the evening; and a recently refurbished small coffee shop near a student hall of residence, which does a great trade during termtime but suffers from an absence of footfall during the generous student holiday periods. One other establishment is flashing bright on our radar. The sales particulars read:

Very popular high turnover independent coffee shop.
Centre of historic Warwickshire town.
Attractively priced for early sale.

The coffee shop that has grabbed our attention is in the town of Kenilworth, Warwickshire. Having learned our lesson, we start our reconnaissance.

Kenilworth is a historic market town with a population of around twenty-five thousand. Its schools are consistently highly rated, its crime rate is low, and its town centre has a mix of independent stores, retailers, pubs, restaurants and coffee shops. There is a strong cultural community thanks to the arts centre and two amateur theatres. When it comes to sports, there is something for everyone – such as golf, cricket, rugby, tennis, squash and croquet. Historic monuments such as Kenilworth Castle and St Mary's Abbey bring many visitors into the town. Thatched cottages, traditional Victorian town houses and modern homes co-exist, and residents are only a short walk from parkland and nature reserves. Nearby towns include Warwick and Leamington Spa, and a twenty-minute drive takes you to Stratford-upon-Avon. Kenilworth is twenty-eighth in the Savills survey of the top fifty places to live in the UK. This survey ranks locations based on the socioeconomic, educational and health profile of the residents. Towns on this list are considered "prime locations". One common characteristic of such places is an attractive and vibrant town centre with independent shops and markets, where people come to shop and socialise – and this footfall feeds the coffee shop businesses.

To my mind, Kenilworth is the sort of place where, if you were to find yourself at the Waitrose checkout without your wallet, a stranger standing in line behind you would be willing to step in to pay for your shopping and trust you to transfer the money when you returned home. As I see it, this is the Kindness of Kenilworth: where young families, working professionals and retirees commingle. On big occasions, such as royal weddings, the main road through the town centre is closed to allow several thousand people to celebrate with a street party. Popular annual events include the firework display, arts festivals and the summer carnival. The Warwickshire Christmas Tractor Run is another annual event guaranteed to bring the community out on the streets. It is organised by the Young Farmers' Club and involves a convoy of around sixty tractors adorned with tinsel and Christmas lights trundling through town. Then there is the Boxing Day rubber duck race, which involves tipping a large collection of rubber ducks (which people have sponsored) into the River Avon and following them to the finishing point. This quirky event has an enthusiastic following and frequently features in the national media. People often talk about living in the 'Kenilworth Bubble': implying that this town is somewhat sheltered from the trials and tribulations of the real world. That may be an accurate statement, but it would be fair to say that the residents of Kenilworth seem to be very welcoming to outsiders like me.

The Facebook group 'Kenilworth Vibes' is a forum for raising and discussing community issues. In common with most community Facebook groups, it has posts relating to lost cats, uncut hedges and local wildlife. There is a strong following for Colin, the white wallaby who lives wild in the woodland around the outskirts of the town. Dog walkers and ramblers often post pictures when they spot him emerging from shrubbery. One issue, causing a significant level of consternation, is a local authority regeneration project, which involves demolishing the one hundred- and twenty-five-year-old Kenilworth Lido. The proposal is to have a modern indoor swimming facility to replace the current complex, which consists of an ageing indoor and outdoor pool. Protests have been organised to prevent this 'travesty.' Other issues discussed on the forum include the council's decision to install bench seating and flowerpots in one of the town centre side streets, without first opening a consultation. Community issues such as these are good for business, as they create a talking point and those with time on their hands will congregate in coffee shops to discuss these and other first-world problems.

The business we are considering purchasing is Arden's Coffee Shop, which is in Talisman Square – a pedestrianised shopping area in the heart of the town. It has a mixture of independent shops and well-known retailers (Boots Opticians, WHSmith). Arden's is in one corner of the square, next door to a jeweller, opposite a florist and approximately fifty metres from a large Waitrose supermarket situated just outside the square. As you stroll from Arden's to the nearby car park, you pass an independent bookshop and a hairdresser before coming to a children's patio garden with an outside piano (sheltered by the canopy). On the upper level, there is a gym and a ladies' fitness studio, Curves.

Unlike The Steam Station, this location has regular footfall.

Within a half-mile radius there are eight other coffee shops, including Costa Coffee at the opposite end of the square. These establishments all seem to do good business, enjoying trade from a combination of loyal regulars and occasional patrons. In short, this is a high-demand, prime location.

Having satisfied ourselves on the suitability of the location, we shift our focus to the viability of the business. The five-page sales particulars go into detail and itemise all equipment, fixtures, fittings and furnishings which are included in the sale. There is a strong client base, a loyalty card scheme, seating for seventy-eight diners inside and another eighteen outside. Offers in the region of £60,000 are invited. For what is described as a high turnover business with consistently rising sales, this seems too good to be true. It further states, 'genuine personal reason for sale.'

That purchase price is within our budget, but the annual rent is £30,000, business rates are £10,000 and the annual service charge is in the region of £2,500. This type of lease moves us into a whole new ballpark as the annual rent for The Steam Station was £10,000 and business rates £2,000. Nevertheless, this coffee shop has an annual net turnover of £360,000 and has been steadily growing since its formation ten years ago. This could be viewed as a daunting and high-risk undertaking, but there is so much in its favour. The asking price has been set on the basis that the current owner is looking for a quick sale and a reliable buyer (i.e., a cash purchase). He currently runs the business with his daughter; she was planning to take over the business but has since decided to pursue a different career path.

We arrange a viewing. It is a one-hour drive from my house. Kieran doesn't drive and it is two hours' travel time for him from his home in Birmingham.

We meet at the premises on Friday, late in the afternoon. The sale is confidential, so viewings must take place after the staff go home. There is a 5-star food hygiene rating sticker on the front door. The owner, Jon, welcomes us, and we shake hands, which feels a bit awkward as we've only recently relaxed social distancing rules. We get a guided tour, he describes day-to-day operations and talks us through some of the routine maintenance tasks, such as deep cleaning the ice cream machine. The shop is extraordinarily well-equipped: ice maker, blenders, milkshake whiskers, two full-height double freezers, multiple refrigerators, bake-off oven, speed-oven, salad bar, panini grill, commercial dishwasher, back-up dishwasher, back-up coffee machine, three large digital menu displays. The furnishings and décor are a bit dated — dark laminate countertop and bright, red-coloured furnishings – it feels like a 1990s style Costa Coffee time capsule. Nevertheless, redecoration and furnishings seem inconsequential, and I suspect Sharon will have an opinion on colour schemes and furnishings.

I make some mental calculations and conclude that if I were to fit out this premises with new equipment and furniture, to the current specification, it would cost in the region of £150,000. And this place has just come on the market at £60,000. Importantly, it is a walk-in business, with an established customer base. If this were listed on eBay, I would press *Buy It Now* because I have been sold purely on my value of the equipment and furnishings. This kit may be second-hand, but he has invested in good brands, such as the Merrychef speed oven and a Faema E71 espresso machine. It is a bit like buying a high-mileage Mercedes; it may be out of warranty, but the build quality will help ensure a long and useful lifespan.

I recall our accountant friend Zoe advising us to start small and build up organically; but our circumstances have changed – and when an opportunity like this presents itself, I feel we must move quickly.

Kieran and I are equally enthusiastic, but he couldn't possibly commute from Birmingham to Kenilworth every day.

"If we buy this place, it will mean you and Courtney relocating here," I say.

"I'm okay with that. We'll just need to give one month's notice to our landlord and find somewhere in Kenilworth."

"What about Courtney?"

"Well, she doesn't want to move because she likes being near her family."

"Maybe you can bring her down for a visit. It's a nice town and you'll be earning more money here."

I am aware of other viewings lined up for this business, so I phone the agent on Monday morning and say we wish to purchase it.

"Wouldn't you like to see the accounts for the last three years?" he asks.

"Ah yes, of course I would." I'm aware that is good business sense, but I just want to get in quick in case someone else has an offer accepted and we end up back at our starting point. "I'll ask my accountant to review them," I add.

Our offer is accepted, but my excitement is tinged with despondency as we once again start the legal process. I use the same solicitor. He estimates it will take three months to completion as there are two contracts to execute, one with the vendor who is selling the shop and another with the landlord for reassigning the lease. At least that gives us time to get a business bank account opened.

It's August, three weeks after our offer was accepted and Sharon and I make an incognito visit to the shop on a rainy Saturday afternoon. We park in the Waitrose car park and dash towards the entrance for Arden's. Once inside, I order a latte, soup and a panini, while Sharon has tea and a ciabatta. We go upstairs and sink ourselves into two large tub chairs.

"It's very red," says Sharon.

"I know, but that's just a redecoration job."

"And I'm not keen on these artificial plants." She rubs her thumb and index finger along the outside of one of the leaves.

After five minutes, our order is served to us at the table. Sharon lifts the lid off the tea pot. "Loose-leaf tea. Nice."

"Twelve different teas on the menu," I say.

We finish our food. Sharon visits the toilets, checks out the glossy leaflets pinned to the shop noticeboard and takes in the wall art. We leave and walk around the square, staying under the canopy to keep dry, then head home, feeling content with our purchase.

It's now 1st November, 2021. Eight months have passed since the initial kitchen conversation that started us on this journey, and I have now agreed the contract to purchase Arden's and signed the tenancy agreement. We are now the proud owners of a coffee shop. I announce it on my personal Facebook page and tell my friends about how we got such a good deal on this business.

We invite accountant Zoe and her husband Mark round for celebratory drinks that evening. I forgot to send her copies of the accounts that I received from the agent, although I did read through them myself and verified that the business has been growing profitably over the years, then (like all consumer businesses) lost a lot of trade during the pandemic months and is building up trade once again. Of greater relevance is the recent cash flow, which, according to the owner's accounting system, is showing average gross revenue of £8,000 per week.

We haven't seen Zoe for some time, so I debrief and proudly show them the photo montage on my iPad.

"What the <*swear word*>?" says Zoe, almost spilling her prosecco. "I thought you were buying a small cafe?!"

"That was the plan, but this is a walk-in, ready-to-go business."

"How many covers?" asks Mark.

"Ninety-six across the two floors and outside. But the good thing about this is that some of the staff have been there for years, so I don't need to recruit or train anyone," I say.

"The colour scheme is a bit offensive," says Sharon, "and we need to get rid of those tacky-looking plastic hedges at the entrance door."

"So, how many staff have you taken on?" asks Zoe.

"Eighteen. I've got a listing in a spreadsheet, six full-time and the rest part-time."

"You'll need some help with payroll then," says Zoe, more as a statement of fact than an offer of assistance.

"Some of the part-timers only work at weekends and holiday time," I say.

"Zero- or fixed-hours contracts?"

"A bit of a mixture, I think. A lot of them are students, so I expect a few will leave over the coming months."

"I bloody hope so," she says.

NOVEMBER

My first day of official ownership is Friday 4th November, 2021. I arrive shortly after 7 a.m., and say good morning to the three members of staff on duty, who have already opened up the shop. Lucy is the 'responsible person', who will be managing today. She is twenty-one years old, with long dark hair tied back, manicured nails and flawless makeup. She has a mobile phone squeezed into the back pocket of her dark grey jeans. The other two are Carla and Sarah; all three are wearing black long-sleeved tops with 'Arden's' emblazoned on them in green lettering. Carla is twenty; she started two months ago and seems to still be finding her feet. She is standing alongside Lucy, looking directly at her.

"I've finished setting up the outside tables, what shall I do next?" Carla asks.

"Look, there's the iPad. Just go through the opening checklist," says Lucy.

Carla picks up the iPad and scurries to the opposite end of the counter. Sarah is one of the more experienced staff members and is on kitchen duty today, which means she is responsible for baking scones, setting out the salad bar and making up all the prepare-to-order food that comes through the till. I would estimate her to be between twenty-six and thirty and she works part-time due to her family commitments.

I don't have much in the way of conversation with the team as they are rushing through their morning routines in readiness for opening at 7.30 a.m., such as toilet checks, coffee checks, cash float checked. I wander into the kitchen. The ovens are warming up and the dishwasher is performing its start-up cycle. Sarah is chopping the butter into cubes, presumably for making scones. I walk out of the kitchen into the counter area looking for something useful I can do. The espresso machine hisses to life, and Carla is transferring plastic cartons of milk from the free-standing refrigerator in the middle of the counter area to the smaller refrigerator at the barista station.

"Is there something I can help with?" I ask.

"Not really," says Lucy. "All the regular staff are here. Do you just want us to carry on as usual?"

"Of course, just let me know if there's something you need me to do."

"Oh, the early morning club will be here in a few minutes. They normally get a free coffee on a Friday. They're in every day and always have money on account. Do you want to stick with that?"

"If that's been their arrangement, then let's keep it."

I'm not sure what the early morning club is or how the free coffee on Friday works, but I'm not going to make myself unpopular with customers on my first day.

I take a seat in the customer zone and pull out my laptop. I have a list of suppliers I need to contact today to set up my account and payment terms, the most important ones being those for coffee, food, milk and waste collection. This is necessary admin but I would rather be doing something practical like making coffee or baking scones.

Kieran arrives shortly after 8 o'clock, wearing a face mask and wrapped in a scarf. I introduce him to the team. Lucy hands Kieran a black Arden's T-shirt.

"How long was your journey, Kieran?" I ask.

"Just under two hours. I need to change trains and I walk about two miles to the train station."

"You can't do that every day. Take a taxi to the train station and we'll put it on expenses and hopefully you'll find a place to stay in Kenilworth before Christmas."

I met all the staff three days ago – on the Tuesday – when I started the handover with Jon. The confidentiality of the sale prevailed, and this was the day the staff first learned that he had sold the business and was moving on. I could tell it was a shock for most of them and I expect the long-serving team members, such as Lucy and Sarah, are unsettled by this change of ownership. Jon had built up this business from nothing and has been running it for the last ten years and many of the staff have formed strong bonds with him – a bit like a family.

I spoke to each staff member individually on the Tuesday. My intention was to provide reassurance, but I had a mixed, somewhat underwhelming, response from most, such as:

"I only joined last month, so this change is probably not going to make much difference to me."

"I would like to change my shift patterns, so I just work Monday to Friday. Jon said I should talk to you about that."

"Can you guarantee that nothing is going to change?"

"What do you want with a coffee shop, and why did you buy this place?"

I feel I need to work hard to win their confidence, but I'm also conscious that staffing costs are the highest operational overhead and there will come a time when I will want to reduce this headcount and become more efficient. The staff are all female. In fact, if someone were to attend an all-staff meeting, they would be forgiven for thinking our recruitment policy was biased towards hiring young, slim, attractive females. At least Kieran will add a modicum of diversity.

The final handover tasks occurred last night, which included updating the Point-of-Sale system with my business bank details; this means all card transactions, once accepted by the payment provider, will be transferred to my account daily (minus a 1.2% card processing fee). I gave up with Lloyd's Bank; they were taking too long, and I never knew what the next impediment would be. I started panicking at one point. In all my planning, it never occurred to me that opening a business bank account would be so arduous, and this is one thing I cannot do without. I applied for an account with Tide, who describe themselves as a 'challenger bank'. Identity authentication and business checks were completed within two days, then on the third day I had a fully functional business bank account, which I manage through an app on my smartphone. The one downside is that they do not have any physical branches so I will have to use the Post Office for depositing cash and obtaining change.

To the customers, day one is no different from any other day, as they are served by the same staff and pay the same price for their coffee and food. I introduce myself to some of the morning regulars.

Kieran and I have an early lunch. We sit ourselves outside and our freshly prepared paninis are delivered to our table. A tall, bearded gentleman, carrying a shopping bag, shuffles by, stops, looks at us and says, "The death rate looks like it's going to start rising again." I look around; we are the only ones sitting there.

"Well, I'm keeping hold of my mask," I say. I pull my paper mask out of my jacket pocket and hold it up. He continues to fill us in on the latest pandemic news. I guess Kenilworth is one of these places where random strangers are comfortable striking up a conversation with one another.

As the day goes on, I observe the fast-moving routines of the staff, which run like clockwork. Coffees are delivered to the serving counter; food is dispatched from the kitchen and all orders are served to the customers at their tables. Two additional staff have joined the shift, which makes six team members in total (including Kieran).

I'm invited to sit with three of the daily regulars, who introduce themselves as Gary, Jackie and Sandra. I would estimate them to be in their early seventies. I make the mistake of saying how I appreciate the custom of the elderly regulars.

"We don't use the word 'elderly' in here," says Jackie.

"Are you local?" asks Gary.

"Unfortunately not. I live in Kettering, about forty-five miles away," I say.

"Do you have any other coffee shops?" asks Sandra.

"This is my first, so I'm still learning the trade you could say."

"And what are your plans for this place?" asks Jackie.

"I just want to keep it business as usual, then maybe look at improving a few things. Not sure what yet."

"Well, don't change the coffee," says Gary. He raises his cappuccino cup up and holds it towards me for a second. "Best brew in Kenilworth," he says.

"I'm delighted to hear that." I think about asking him to give us a five-star review on Google but hold back for fear of coming across as pushy, and instead focus on making friends with the customers, whilst observing the staff's operation of serving coffee, cake and food, then cleaning tables afterwards. I overhear the following exchange between customer and staff at the counter:

"I'll have a single-shot latte and carrot cake. Also, Kay will be here in a few minutes, she said she'll have her usual, but I don't know what that is."

"She has a decaf latte, I'll put that through now –" a loyalty card and credit card are handed over – "just take a seat, my lovely, and we'll bring it over to you."

Michelle has been working here for five years. She is a mother and a grandmother, and I would estimate her to be in her mid-forties. She has tattoos on her shoulder and her arm.

She knows all the regulars by name, where they live, who their family members are, where they work (or used to work). She can multitask in a way I would never manage – engaging in social chat while putting orders through on the till and remembering who ordered what drink five minutes before. She comes out on the floor to collect some empties and stops by our table, places her hand on my chair back and sighs.

"Busy today, Michelle?" says Gary.

"I'm knackered." She brushes her forehead. "I haven't even had a fag break yet."

"I think you deserve a pay rise," says Jackie.

"Well, you'd better tell that to my new boss." She nudges her hand into my back.

"What time do you finish, Michelle?" I ask, deftly moving away from a delicate subject.

"Three o'clock, then I need to pick up my youngest from school."

Michelle picks up the empty cups and plates from the table. "More drinks anyone?" she asks. All three order more drinks. She doesn't need to write anything down, just walks back to the counter while singing.

Michelle is the oldest member of staff and the most experienced. She isn't the manager, but she is clearly the cock of the walk in this place.

We close at 4 o'clock. It's been a busy day with takings in the region of twelve hundred pounds. Tomorrow – Saturday – should be even better.

Just before everyone leaves, I call Lucy over. I haven't really had a chance to talk to her, but from what I have seen today, she is a great manager who can assign tasks, predict where the next rush is coming from, multitask with the espresso machine and still have friendly exchanges with the customers. The less experienced staff look to her for direction. It would be great if she and Kieran could work in partnership to manage this place. She sits down opposite me, a laptop between us.

"Looks like it's been a good day," I say.

"It was quite stressful. One of the staff had to cut short her lunch break and help Sarah in the kitchen because we had a mad lunchtime rush," she says.

"I wish I could have jumped in and helped, but I would have probably just got in the way."

"We're short-staffed," she says, "we need at least two more people who are coffee trained or food-prep trained. We can't even cover the staff lunch breaks on days like this."

"OK, well, I was planning to look at the staffing more generally, and Kieran will be up to speed soon."

"Well, I'm going on holiday for a week at the end of the month and I don't think we have cover."

"Point taken." She wasn't going to let this drop. "Tell you what, let me write up a job advert tonight and post it tomorrow."

She stays for twenty minutes and pushes me to tell her what my plans are for this place. I raise the question of making the place more efficient and she remains focussed on getting more staff trained up, "otherwise our standards are going to drop," she says.

She stands up to leave. "Are you coming in tomorrow?" she asks.

"Of course. I want to meet the Saturday staff and see if I can do more to help."

I reflect on my first day with perplexity. It's as if I have parachuted myself in as captain of an ocean-going liner in mid-voyage, only to realise I have little awareness of nautical navigation and there is no opportunity to disembark. I must rely entirely on the ship's crew and my biggest fear now is losing key team members. Lucy is one of those people. She is the highest paid, but I don't want her to leave and will increase her salary if necessary.

Two weeks in, and my first fortnight has been one of disorder and distraction. Rather than building a plan for growth and efficiency, I find myself continually running into roadblocks and time-consuming diversions. I have received a resignation email from one of the staff because she doesn't want to work on Saturdays anymore. I had declined her request as we already have two permanent staff with that privilege, and we need the fastest and most experienced people working on Saturdays. Another member of staff informed me she is pregnant. This means I need to write up a risk assessment and ensure her working conditions are safe. Our wholesale food supplier – Wheelers – has been making deliveries twice a week at a cost of approximately £700 for each delivery, but they are unable to continue this service because I don't have a customer account with them. The problem is, they aren't taking on new customers in this locality due to a driver shortage. I make what I consider to be a reasonable argument along the lines of "I'm taking over an existing account and simply want the same service we've always had." After numerous telephone conversations, they finally agree to give me an account and resume deliveries. In the week of no deliveries, I had to make frequent shopping trips to the cash-and-carry, six miles away.

Our waste collection occurs twice weekly, though this went down to once a week after I signed the new service agreement with the company responsible for waste collection. OK, perhaps it's my fault for not reading the service level agreement diligently, but I did verbally ask for the same level of service. This resulted in overflowing waste, which is a violation of health and safety rules. I managed to transport the large quantities of cardboard to the recycling centre, and that freed up space.

I find myself having to make decisions, such as what our Christmas opening hours should be and who is working on what days. Staff advise me that mornings are quiet over the holiday period, and they are happy when I agree to a later opening time (10 a.m. rather than 7.30 a.m.). The staff roster keeps changing due to the family and party commitments of the staff. One wants to know if she's working, so she can 'get pissed' safe in the knowledge she's not working the next day.

I have not had the time to get too involved in operational work, and I try not to encumber the team with my questions or instructions and just leave them to their routines. I love the fact that the staff and regulars know each other by name, and this makes for cordial and efficient customer service. Kieran is fitting into the team well, has learned the shop operating procedures and is now making scones, preparing food and doing barista duty.

Sharon came in at the start of our second week and within thirty minutes, knew more about the staff than I did. That day, I learned that one is a qualified beauty consultant, and another is an amateur singer. Sharon has also taken the initiative to organise a Christmas party. I love this idea as I'm not convinced the staff have fully accepted us yet. I've heard comments about standards dropping and "it's not the same as it used to be." I'm hoping the Christmas party will be a good team bonding session.

I am three weeks into ownership and I'm now splitting my time between coffee shop work and my regular job. This means I'm often found sitting upstairs with my laptop open and headset on, and this is exactly where I am today. There's a lady sitting at the other end of the room who is also remote working using her mobile phone. She has earphones but her voice carries. She appears to be part of an online meeting. A cappuccino is served to her at the table. Almost two hours later, she is still there, but has made herself more comfortable by sitting sideways on the sofa with her back leaning on the armrest and her feet up. She hasn't ordered anything further and her cappuccino cup has long since been cleared away. Other customers have been and gone, but no one has complained – perhaps out of politeness. I've decided to go home. I close my laptop and try to catch her eye on the way out, but she is oblivious to everything except her smartphone.

I arrive at 8 o'clock the next morning and walk into the middle of a staff conversation about a rude customer who had been in the shop the previous day.

"Then she pointed her finger at me and said she has a really important meeting and it's my fault that she can't do it," says Lucy. "She had a go at Carla too and got quite aggressive because we wouldn't charge her phone. All the customers were looking at her."

"What did she look like?" I ask, although that is a pointless question as it couldn't be anyone else. It turns out her phone had run out of battery power, she wanted a charging cable, and wasn't prepared to accept any excuse for us not providing this service.

"I told her we don't have any charging cables," says Lucy.

"She could have gone to WHSmith and bought one," I say.

"Well, she just stood there and told us she had a very important job, and I was stopping her from doing it. Then she stormed out," says Lucy.

There is a breed of person who seems to think that because they're a paying customer, it gives them licence to bully those who serve them. Coffee shops are normally places of happy conversation and friendly exchanges between customers and staff. Unexpected hostility such as this is one sure way of creating a *bad day at work* experience, which in this case has carried on to the next day. If there is one thing I could change about the hospitality industry, it would be the introduction of a Bad Manners Tax for obnoxious customers.

By the end of my first month, I've got to know many of the regular customers, such as the gentlemen who make up the early morning club, the school dads and the local traders and professionals – the builders, Elliot the Horticulturalist, the personal trainers from the gym, the hairdressers, sports shop staff, the Eastern European gentlemen and all the daytime regulars.

My confidence levels are improving in small increments day by day, although I am conscious of certain key tasks I've either completely avoided or delegated. I haven't laid a finger on the espresso machine; staff scheduling is under the control of the managers, and I haven't done any bookkeeping or even set up my chart of accounts on my accounting system (I'm using Xero accounting). Zoe has already warned me to do bank reconciliation *every day* and to keep on top of cash flow. For the time being, the important items are being done – I'm paying invoices directly through bank transfer and my first staff salary payments have gone through without error, thanks to a bureau service I subscribed to. Once I get some headspace, I will learn all about payroll and do the job myself.

It's Friday 10th December, and it's Christmas party night. I've booked two tables at the Chesford Grange Hotel, who host celebration events, with a disco every Friday and Saturday evening in December. This seems to raise excitement levels in the shop, especially amongst the student weekend staff. A couple of them asked what they should wear. I suggested a nice frock; I've always found that to be a good general answer to a female dress code question.

We meet in the bar at 7 p.m. for drinks, then at 7.30, we are ushered into the party venue with two hundred other people –

office workers, schoolteachers, hospital staff –forming an eclectic mix of revellers. There are twenty or so tables which accommodate several staff parties from different companies. Everyone takes their seats. Wine is poured, Christmas crackers are pulled, paper hats are adorned, reindeer and snowman jokes are shared, and the hall echoes with conversations and laughter. There are seventeen of us from Arden's; the hotel has prepared name cards, and everyone takes their seats at one of our two assigned tables. I've pre-ordered mid-priced bottles of wine and beer, which have been delivered to our tables, but a couple of the girls go to the bar to buy spirit drinks. The DJ starts proceedings with an elimination competition to guess the year of the song. Bottles of fizz are awarded to the winning and second-place tables, and we come a respectable third place.

After dinner, the DJ takes his position behind the turntable and high-energy dance music booms out of the two large speakers at each end of the stage. I see Lucy making her way to the dance floor, the younger girls following her. Some people remain at their table, others leave their seats to mingle with friends on other tables – it has all the elements of a fun-filled Christmas party.

Midway through the evening, I notice several empty seats at our table. Michelle has had to go home early (as planned), which leaves me and Sharon; directly opposite are Kieran and Courtney. Those who were seated with us are now crammed around the other Arden's table, adjacent to ours, but beyond talking distance. They are all in good spirits, enjoying the vibrant atmosphere and their own conversations. My idea of a new-team bonding night is not playing out as I'd hoped. The metaphorical group hug I was hoping for has flatlined. I don't think it is a personal snub; more an indicator of a tight-knit team, who have not yet accepted their new leadership.

SETTLING IN

I t's the 17th of December. Sharon and I had hoped to have started the upstairs refurbishment, but other priorities have emerged, such as the impending visit from the health and food safety inspector. He is due next week for a registration visit. I'm not sure what that involves, so I intend to spend my available time reading up on the regulations, completing online training and doing walkaround cleanliness checks.

Our seasonal menu is proving popular, especially the luxury mince pies with cream and speciality hot chocolates, like orange and honeycomb. Kieran is fitting into his role as one of the managers, and I am enjoying getting to know the regular customers. There is a happy Christmas vibe in the shop. We have put up lights and decorations, switched the background music to festive playlists and there are around twelve Christmas cards on display above the counter, all of them from customers, written out to, 'All the wonderful staff at Arden's'.

We have hired one new part-time team member, but I have been reminded, yet again, that, "we still need more staff as there are gaps in the rota due to upcoming holidays." For the time being, my priority is to ensure smooth continuity of service, so I acquiesce to the demands for increased headcount and decide to come back to the efficiency problem later.

I've been trying to stamp a bit of my own identity onto this newly acquired business, so have invested in new staff uniforms — t-shirts and sweat tops. I've kept them black, but I've created a new logo, so each top now has, *'Arden's super hero,'* imprinted in white lettering. I bought enough for all the current staff and all future recruits. Kieran and the new staff member are wearing the new tops, but Lucy, Carla, Sarah and a few others are still wearing their original tops, with the old logo. I wonder if they are still holding on to the way things used to be. Perhaps I'm overthinking this.

It's Monday, which means the manager on duty and another staff member spend the morning placing orders for the week's supplies, which includes food ingredients, cakes, coffee beans, loose-leaf tea, syrups, hot chocolates, smoothie pouches, porridge pots, takeaway packaging and cleaning supplies. It takes two staff three hours to do this as it involves counting the current stock levels and purchasing the right quantities from multiple suppliers, whilst being mindful not to overstock (due to limited storage space). This is one routine I'm sure can be optimised. I recall our consultants – Andrew and Claire – advising us to do weekly stocktaking.

I know we can use our Point-of-Sale system for this, but we don't enter our deliveries or stock levels into it. If we did, then the weekly ordering process could be almost automated. That's a job for another day.

We have had a good response from the job advert we posted on the 'Indeed' recruitment portal. When it comes to front-of-house hospitality, customers value staff who are naturally friendly and courteous. So, I have created a shortlist of candidates we think have the personality attributes to fit into the team and I'm now scheduling interviews.

Sharon and I are conducting the interviews; we have seen two already today and we have another scheduled for now. We walk downstairs together to meet the next candidate – Deborah. She is sitting at a table by the counter talking to two of the staff, and it looks like she's making a good impression. I would estimate her to be around thirty years of age. Tall, slim, shoulder-length blonde hair and wearing a long, beige-coloured coat. Attractive, well-presented and with an engaging presence: more like someone who would be serving in an upmarket wine bar rather than a coffee shop.

"Leave this interview to me," Sharon says.

We all head upstairs. I camp out at my work desk in a corner space behind a partition, where there is just enough room for me and my laptop. I may be tucked away, but I'm still able to hear what's going on.

Sharon has a different style of interviewing to me. She goes more for the subjective big-picture questions such as, "What has been your greatest achievement?" or "Where do you see yourself in five years' time?" I wouldn't be surprised if her next questions is something like, "If you were a garden flower, what season would you bloom in?" Twenty minutes in and she finally gets to the relevant questions: "How many staff were you managing in your previous job?" Then, she comes good with this simple question,

"Why do you want to go back to working in a coffee shop?"

"I love coffee and talking to people about coffee. I've organised coffee -tasting experiences before. I like to describe the different taste profiles from regional beans, such as sweetness and the taste sensations such as chocolate and spice."

She knows her coffee. I creep out from behind the partition as she starts to describe the difference between Arabica and Robusta beans and how to get a balance between strength and bitterness by adjusting the grind. Deborah is clearly an experienced manager with good organisational skills and connects well with people, but what she has just described is a masterclass for the coffee connoisseur. She is overqualified for the role we are recruiting for, but ideas are forming in my head. She could be our coffee ambassador. We could organise tasting sessions and have her talk about different varieties. She knows how to hold an audience. The early morning club would love this, so would the school dads and the builders. This could also be a springboard for our retail business – selling speciality coffee beans.

We say goodbye and promise to be in touch soon. Sharon and I have our debrief.

"She's the best one yet," says Sharon.

"Agree. But overqualified for the barista job. I'm not saying I don't want her, just a statement of fact, we'd have to pay her a bit more."

"She can be a manager. She made a good impression with the staff earlier on."

"That's because they thought she would be a barista. Making her manager is like putting another cock in the henhouse. She would still have to learn shop operations from the existing staff, then she would be their boss. We would have to be here to help manage the fallout from the others, who think they should be manager," I say.

"Well, we have two more left to interview tomorrow, so let's think it over before making a decision."

Next day, I interview two more people. One of them – Patricia – has previously worked in Starbucks. She is a softly-spoken, blonde twenty-two-year-old, who comes across as customer-friendly and is looking for thirty hours a week. She is the perfect fit for the barista role, and in budget. She accepts the position and gives her current employer one week's notice. We feel she will be a great addition to the team, although with Kieran being the only male, we still lack gender diversity.

Deborah would have been a great hire, especially as manager, but we're not ready for her just yet, and she would have cost at least £2.00 more per hour than an experienced barista. Then there is the challenge of managing team dynamics, as others would feel overlooked. Throw in the privilege of being coffee ambassador, and that would be like pouring salt on the wounds.

It is Wednesday, 22nd December and I'm expecting a visit from the local authority health inspector. If my understanding is correct, the purpose of a registration visit is to give us an initial assessment of our hygiene and food safety procedures. The Food Standards Agency (FSA) has defined a rating scale from 0 to 5. I have been fortunate to take over a shop with a hygiene rating of 5, which had been issued some years previously. Sadly, this is not transferable upon change of ownership, which means I must go through a two-stage inspection process from scratch. Today's registration visit is a bit like a mock exam. The official rating will be determined after an unannounced inspection at some future point in time.

The regulations are strong on areas such as allergy management, temperature monitoring, staff training and food labelling. We have systems in place for all of this and we have done a bit of a deep clean in the kitchen over the last two days, including getting into the hard-to-reach areas such as the two-inch gap between the freezer and the wall – which has evidently been neglected for some time.

Robert arrives at 10 a.m. as scheduled. He is a tall gentleman whom I would estimate to be in his fifties. He is carrying a brief-case in one hand and has an identity badge dangling from a lan-yard around his neck. We go upstairs as it is quieter there and start by completing a registration form which captures details on the business, including the types of food and beverages we sell and what we prepare on the premises. He asks how we record details of allergens for the food we sell, and I explain that every item on our menu is entered into our Nutritics system, which is available to customers through a touchscreen display positioned at the front of the counter. I show him our latest pest control report and the training certificates of those staff who work on food preparation in the kitchen. He nods his approval and takes pictures. I stumble a bit when I try to explain how we can view historical temperature records for refrigeration. I grab one of the shop iPads and pull up a live graphical display which shows the current temperature of each freezer and refrigerator, but I never really use this and when I work out how to view the history, it shows a temporary sensor failure on one of the freezers.

We move downstairs as he wants to see the kitchen and serving space. On the way down, I point to the customer allergy display monitor. Unfortunately, the screen is frozen and is simply showing an empty web browser page. I prod the screen repeatedly, but it is unresponsive. "I probably just need to restart it," I say.

"Do you have the allergy information at the till?" he asks.

"Michelle," I call out to the counter area, "can you show Robert how you tell customers about allergens?" If Michelle doesn't know how to do this, then we're in trouble.

"It's all in the till system." She walks back over to the till. "I just need to search for the food, press the 'more details' button and it's listed here." She points to the till touchscreen. Robert is writing in his notebook. We move into the kitchen. Kieran explains the food labelling system. Every time a food item is removed from the fridge or freezer, the team selects the item from the wall mounted digital display, which is pre-programmed with use-by dates, and a food label is printed from a separate device.

He continues writing in his notebook. "Can you show me your bin store?"

"Let me grab the key," I say.

We leave via the back kitchen door and walk towards the outside bin store, which hosts a 1,000-litre flip-top bin and a smaller 240-litre bin. I explain that our bins fill up quickly, especially after a delivery, but we have a contract in place with a private company who do two collections a week. I insert the key, turn the lock and swing open both wooden doors and two food waste bags fall out at our feet. The bin is overflowing, and the floor is strewn with empty bottles, food waste and cardboard packaging. I don't need a Level 2 health and safety certificate to tell me this is a hygiene risk.

"I cannot believe this." I just stare at it, then look back up at him. "This should have been emptied yesterday," I say.

He pulls out his smartphone and takes a picture. "A lot of places have driver shortages just now due to absence. You probably want to talk to your contractor about different collection days," he says.

We go back inside, and he finishes by looking in all the cupboards behind the counter. He has a particular interest in the ice cream maker – a large stainless-steel machine, with a dispensing lever protruding from its front panel. It sits atop the counter, alongside a tower of cones and a compartmented box of assorted toppings. He takes a picture of it. We go back upstairs, where he summarises everything and offers advice on industry resources, staff training and allergy management.

"I will write up these recommendations and send them over to you," he says, "then next step is a formal inspection, which is unannounced, but it will be no sooner than six weeks from now."

We shake hands and say goodbye. I thank all the staff. Despite the bin store debacle, they had done a great job of showing we are a hygiene and safety-conscious workplace. I just wish I knew when the official inspection was going to take place.

We are between Christmas and New Year and our shop is opening at 10 a.m. instead of 7.30 a.m. for three midweek days. On the last of these days, I come in early to do some equipment maintenance. I'm dismantling the ice cream-dispensing machine to perform its monthly deep clean while reading the manual, which is lying open on the floor. I hear a knock on the window. I look up. It's still dark outside and I see three of the men from the early morning club peering through the window. Graham is holding both arms out, palms up, as if to say, "What's going on?" I dash to the door.

"I'm so sorry," I say, "we're opening later this week because of the Christmas holidays."

"Well, we're still working as normal," says Graham. I would say he is in his early sixties; as usual, he is dressed in a two-piece suit with a perfectly ironed shirt and tie. "Can't you just serve us coffee?"

"I wish I could, but I don't know how to operate the coffee machine." I'm starting to feel embarrassed at my inability to do the one thing the shop relies on most. "I've told the staff we'll open at 10 a.m. for these three days, as we thought it would be quieter than usual."

"Do you know, people have been queueing up outside Waitrose since six o'clock this morning." He points towards the superstore. "They've got a sale on. You've missed out on some good business there."

"I didn't think of that."

"You work in computing, don't you?" says Graham.

"Yes, that's my other job – and I'm still getting the hang of running this business," I say, by means of apologetic explanation.

"We've had to go to Costa these last two days. I can't stand their coffee. Yours is a hundred times better."

I apologise again, lock the door and watch as the three disgruntled gentlemen walk towards the other end of the square towards their second-choice coffee shop.

There are normally five of them who arrive within a few minutes of each other at opening time every morning; their order is a cortado, flat white, cappuccino and two lattes. They sit in the same spot – two on the sofa, the others on chairs – and spend half an hour or so shooting the breeze ahead of their working day. Sometimes, they order a second round of drinks and occasionally they are joined by one or two ladies and other friends. They get a freebie on a Friday – an arrangement put in place by the previous owner, which I have not rescinded yet as I value their custom.

It turns out that theirs isn't the only loyalty I've damaged. Steve and Simon – two more morning regulars – came in at lunchtime, saw me and asked why I'm not open at the normal time these days. "We had to go to Costa and drink crap coffee," said Simon. I tell them I'm not going to change the opening times again, give them both a free drink, and all is forgiven.

I recall many years ago coming across a marketing concept known as the four Ps (product, place, price and promotion). The general idea is that all four elements contribute to the customer's purchasing decision. Costa is less than two hundred yards away; they charge the same as us for coffee and have better promotions due to their recognisable brand identity. However, for these customers, it is the quality of that product that is the deciding factor in where to go for their morning ritual and the fact they have chosen Arden's is reassuring. Hopefully, we won't disappoint them again.

I remind myself to prioritise learning how to operate our machine and make a decent latte. I would love to spend some time behind the counter on barista duty, but, as a rule, everyone who prepares coffees must be trained and be able to demonstrate how to make all the espresso-based drinks to a consistent high standard. I'm not there yet.

JANUARY

We are into the first week of the new year and I have a nagging concern that I don't know how much operational profit we have made in these first two months. Ultimately, I'm aiming for £3,000 a month, which should be achievable as our takings at the till amount to something in the region of £34,000 a month. On day one, I deposited £20,000 into the business bank account to ensure we had enough to pay immediate bills. At the end of December, after doing payroll and settling all outstanding bills, the balance stands at £27,170. However, I haven't yet been invoiced for next quarter's rent or calculated our VAT liability. There are probably other costs which need to be allocated, but the truth is, I haven't had time to learn the basics of bookkeeping or get my head round the accounting system. Zoe would be horrified, but the fact is there have been so many other time-demanding tasks competing for my limited bandwidth, not least my regular job. Nevertheless, allowing for one-off costs, such as uniforms and bills still to be invoiced, I estimate we are generating around £1,500 monthly profit, which I'm happy with, so long as we can build on that through efficiency savings and increased revenue, such as Sunday opening.

As I reflect back on the disorderly learning journey of the last two months, I conclude that, although there is still much to do, we are on an upward trajectory. Two new staff members have been onboarded, Kieran and Courtney have relocated from Brimingham to Kenilworth, and Courtney is due to commence working here within the next week. I've made friends with some of the regular customers, such as Kirk, who is a fitness trainer at a nearby gym and Sharon has linked up with the Kenilworth artists community and we have agreed that they can have a permanent art display in our upstairs space. Our other plans are to open on a Sunday, do some barista training, refurbish the upstairs space and work on operational efficiency. Sharon has a desire to obtain a licence to sell alcohol and foresees a healthy market for prosecco cocktails, especially during summer.

I haven't yet worked out the right balance of time at home and time in the coffee shop. It would be nice to have a regular pattern, but when I am needed in the shop, it's normally at a moment's notice. Today, I'm working at home. It's 9.30 a.m. and I receive a message on WhatsApp from Sarah, the manager on duty.

"Nicky has just gone home because she's scared of catching COVID."

"Really? What brought that on?" I ask.

"Cathy [one of the part-time girls] has just received a phone call from a relative she was staying with over Christmas, and apparently the relative tested positive for COVID and Nicky says she is uncomfortable working around her."

"Has Cathy taken a test, or does she have symptoms?"

"She's taken a test and it's negative and she feels fine, but Nicky got into a panic and said she had to leave."

"That seems like an overreaction," I say.

"That means we're short-handed again today. I've not done the supplier orders yet," she says.

"Okay, let me contact her."

Nicky only started with us about a month ago and has been a great team member. I go to my email and a message appears in bold at the top of my inbox. It's from Nicky. She apologises for walking out and goes on to explain that she has recently found out she is pregnant, which came as a shock, and she has many worries, but "catching COVID is a huge worry … my main priority is to protect myself and baby … This means I need to risk-assess every situation."

Brilliant! I now have two pregnant team members. That's not something I had planned for in the early stages of ownership; I'll need to prepare another maternity plan and think about maternity cover when the time comes. I respond to say congratulations and ask if she has been vaccinated. She replies to say she has and had a booster on Christmas Eve to "protect myself further." I reply in a conciliatory manner, stating that she should take the precautions that she feels are appropriate for her situation.

A renewed phase of pandemic panic is starting to take hold across the country due to the emergence of a new COVID variant – Omicron – which is rumoured to be resistant to vaccines. In recent months, the country has been cautiously edging back to normality, but two years of chaos and anxiety are still fresh in everyone's mind so precautionary reactions like this are to be expected, I guess. Like most other hospitality business owners, I live in hope that we don't have a full-scale phase two pandemic with further lockdowns.

I receive the anticipated letter from the health and food safety authority as a follow-up from the registration visit just before Christmas. The first line I read states, *The general level of compliance with the legislation was found to be satisfactory.* That's a good start, I think. *However, improvements should be made . . .* It went on to list the areas to be addressed, such as fixing a hygienic door handle to a cupboard, reviewing our allergen management system, using independent probe thermometers and reviewing the waste collection schedule. There is nothing complicated in the list; it's just more jobs for me to do. As this was a registration visit, a food rating has not been issued; but, if one were, I estimate it would have been a 3 – Satisfactory. This is good news, but I would like to aim higher than that. It would be helpful if I knew when the official inspection will take place – it may be six weeks or six months. The chances are, I'm not going to be there when he next turns up, so I need to make sure all managers are briefed and, in the meantime, I will prioritise fixing the problems that were listed.

It's late afternoon on a Thursday, and I'm on a video meeting with people from my regular job. There are six of us in the video call, all working from a non-office location. Two people have bookcases as backdrops, and they appear to be stocked with what looks like a carefully curated collection of intellectual books. Another is sitting at her kitchen island. I seem to be the only one sitting in a coffee shop. No one has commented on my backdrop of artwork and artificial plants. I'm thankful that the flexible home-working arrangements are very much still the norm for my employer because I feel I need to be ever-present to deal with day-to-day issues, such as suppliers delivering the wrong goods, staff scheduling problems, and recruitment. I finish my conference call and switch my focus to my neglected email inbox. I hear the clatter of the outside seating being stacked downstairs, which normally signals the end-of-day cleaning routine is in progress. Lucy and Sarah appear at the top of the stairs. They walk towards me; it doesn't look as though they are here to vacuum.

"Steve, we'd like to talk to you," says Lucy. She is holding what looks like a long shopping list. "Our standards are dropping, and I think we're going to start losing customers because we don't have the quality we used to have."

I pull my hands behind my head and clasp my hands together and exhale. "Okay. What's the problem and what do we need to do to fix it?" I say.

"We've put together a list of things that are bringing our standards down."

They walk me through their list, taking it in turns to read out each item – defrosted paninis left in an unsealed box, used cleaning cloth left on the counter overnight, someone opened a second bag of decaffeinated beans without finishing off the bag that was already opened.

"When I came in this morning, there were no muffins defrosted and none on display and you've seen how rushed we are first thing," says Sarah.

"OK, it sounds like people are making mistakes." I nod my head in acknowledgement. "But I'm relying on you two to train and set standards. I've noticed the condiment stations get missed with cleaning sometimes. Also, how about you doing some one-to-one training? Just to get them up to the right standard," I say.

"We don't have the time," says Sarah.

"Also, the quality of the coffee isn't the same," says Lucy.

"I drink the coffee and I see what is being served and there's nothing wrong with it. The customers still tell me they love it," I say.

"Jon used to sign off people before they could serve coffee. We care about this place, and we don't want to see it going downhill," says Lucy.

We continue talking about mistakes, but I'm sensing this conversation is just a symptom of a deeper issue. Their list of infringements seems like an overreaction to trivial mistakes that often arise from inexperience. Sarah and Lucy can run this operation with their eyes closed, and still deal with day-to-day disruptions, but they seem to be missing the old Arden's. The familiarity and security they once had has been swept away and replaced with uncertainty. My initial feeling of exasperation gives way to a sympathetic understanding of how they are feeling. They probably feel put-upon, especially as Kieran has stepped up into a manager role. I remind myself to be more empathetic and sensitive to the emotional impact that changes of this nature can have on people.

It's already dark outside when I close my laptop. I'm looking forward to getting home. I'm about to slip into my coat when Chloe – another team member – appears at the top of the stairs and walks towards me. "Steve, can I have a chat?"

"Sure." I gesture my hand towards the seat opposite. I have a feeling she's going to ask for a pay rise.

"You said you would look at changing my shift patterns when you first took over," she says.

"Yes, I remember. Sorry, it's just been so busy since then."

"I would like to not work Saturdays anymore. I've got family commitments. So, can you change my hours to Monday to Friday?

The same as Michelle and Sarah?"

I shake my head. "Saturday's our busiest day, I can't just switch you to Monday to Friday," I say. Chloe is a very direct person, so I feel I need to be similarly direct. Her head droops in disappointment.

"What about Sarah and Michelle?"

"They're both part-time and their working pattern is what was in place before I took over," I say.

The conversation ends at that point. I'm not quite sure what she means by family commitments as she lives with her parents and doesn't have any children (to my knowledge).

Next day, in the evening, I receive an email of resignation from Chloe. I have mixed feelings about this. She is a good barista, but not suited to hospitality. There have been complaints about her, 'being rude' to customers. She also selfishly stays on the barista station rather than rotating to the floor or kitchen. I don't think the staff will miss her. I wonder if I can replace her with a part-time team member.

We are now in mid-January. Thankfully, the new COVID variant has not taken hold as feared and the daily death toll, as reported on the news, continues to fall. Government guidance on social distancing and cross-border travel have been relaxed. Nevertheless, people are still cautious, and many customers continue to wear face masks. I have just issued new guidance to all staff, which is in line with the updated government recommendations, as follows:

When working in the kitchen or behind the counter, you are not required to wear a face covering. However, you should feel free to continue to wear one if you feel more comfortable doing so.

When the shop is busy and you are serving customers at tables, you should wear a face covering.

As before, if you have COVID symptoms or have tested positive, you should not come to work.

Other safety protections we have in place include hand sanitisers at the entrance and Perspex screens at the counter to protect staff and customers from transmission of infectious droplets. We also have hardboard dividers between some of the seating spaces. These are black hardwood boards, approximately five feet high and three feet wide. Each is affixed to a window frame and the floor to create a partition between the six window tables. However, this means people sit with their backs to them, so, as far as I can see, they serve no practical purpose, and are simply symbols of precaution. After closing on Wednesday evening, I unscrew them from their fasteners and consign them to the bin store. The downstairs seating is instantly improved by their removal as there is more space to move around; there should also be more sunlight radiating through the windows.

Next day, whilst I'm at home, I receive a message from Kieran to say that two separate people have complained about our removal of the boards that separate the window tables.

"Okay, just tell them it is in line with government guidance and, by the way, no other coffee shop in Kenilworth has them," was my reply. I feel he could have dealt with that on his own.

It's Saturday 20th January and I arrive at the shop shortly after 9 a.m. As I enter, a couple are about to leave – a tall, heavy-built man in his fifties and his lady partner, half his size. I hold the door open for them. "Thank you," I say as he's about to leave.

He stops, and turns towards me. "You're the owner, aren't you?" he says, at high volume.

"That's right." I smile, thinking he's going to tell me how much he loves our coffee.

"I'm feeling a lot less safe since you've taken down those boards." He points to the window tables.

"But they weren't really doing anything to protect people," I say.

He shakes his head and walks out the door, then looks back at me and bellows, "I don't feel as safe coming in here anymore."

I'm beginning to realise how strongly some people feel about visible virus protection.

Hopefully it will be forgotten about in a few days. I pull on a face mask and start clearing tables. It's mid-morning, and I'm happy to see the shop getting busy. I emerge from the kitchen into the customer area. The first person I bump into is someone we know as Moaning Minnie. A slim lady, I would estimate to be around thirty years old, with long straight blonde hair. The lower half of her face is covered by a face mask; she is standing back from the counter, waiting on her takeaway order. I believe she works in a local beautician's and comes in frequently for takeaway coffee. She is generally impatient and always makes time for a complaint, such as the cup being too full and causing her to spill the coffee. Today, she must think she's hit the jackpot as she has something to complain about just when I cross her line of sight, providing her with the ideal target for her wrath.

"That girl should be wearing a mask," she says, pointing to Fiona, who is serving at the till.

"It's okay, that Perspex screen stops person-to-person transmission. Only when staff are serving at tables do they need to wear masks," I say. I can only see the top half of her face but I can tell by her eyes and her furiously flapping, heavily mascaraed eyelashes, that she is shocked at my casual attitude to face masks.

"She would never be able to do that in my shop. Everyone needs to wear a mask. She could spread it to someone else and they would spread it out here."

"I'm just trying to be practical, and they've mostly all been vaccinated, so there really is little risk," I continue.

She points towards Fiona. "She should be sent home if she refuses to wear a mask."

I remind myself of my role as a hospitality owner talking to a customer and dial back my argumentative impulses. "I'm just aligning with government guidelines, but let me look at it again," I say, as I retreat to the kitchen.

I get through the remainder of the day without any further confrontation but I'm learning a bruising lesson about the perception of safety precautions for some customers.

Next day, I re-affix the separation boards – five of them with their long edge fastened to the window frame and the floor edge secured to the floor with extra-strong tape. The window tables are once again separated by these unsightly black panels, which means customers can sit with their backs to them, safe in the knowledge that any airborne droplets with a sense of spatial navigation will not transmit through the panels.

THE REFURBISHMENT

There is an art and craft fair in Talisman Square, made up of a diverse range of stalls, selling watercolour art, ceramics, handmade gift cards and portrait drawings, all produced by creatively minded people from the Kenilworth locality. Sharon and I are walking round all the stalls seeking inspiration for our redecoration plans. We are drawn to the works of an artistic photographer who has several framed images on display, such as one of a full moon dominating a cloudless skyline and another of an early morning scene of low-lying mist on Abbey Fields. The stall holder is a lady in her mid-thirties. She is wearing a long new-age-style scarf wrapped around her neck and a matching woolly hat and gloves.

"Are you looking for a gift or is it for yourself?" she asks. The market has just opened, and we are her only potential customers. She smiles at us and claps her hands together. I guess she's looking to make her first sale of the day.

"Actually, we're looking for ideas for decorating our coffee shop," I reply.

"We've just bought Arden's." Sharon points to our shop, which is about fifty metres away.

"Congratulations," she says. "When do you open?"

"We are open, look." I point to the shop. "You can see customers through the window. There's two people walking in now."

"Have you ever been in?" asks Sharon.

She shakes her head in quick bursts. "It's a bit soulless and characterless, isn't it?"

"Many people like what we do," I say. "I had a customer tell us this morning that we have the best hot chocolate in Kenilworth."

"You should pop in today if you get a chance," adds Sharon.

"No thanks. I've got a flask of tea." She points to the flask and mug sitting on her table.

We move on without making a purchase. I was initially hoping to engage her in conversation about adding to our art display in the coffee shop, but I think that would have been a wasted conversation. Although it is good to get some direct feedback, even if it was *direct*.

Sharon and I are back in the shop, sitting upstairs and discussing redecoration options and priorities. We are each sitting on a dark-brown tub chair with a Formica-topped table separating us. We have fluorescent tube lighting and some down lamps with large dome-shaped paper lampshades. The red, wooden-framed sofas blend in with the black-and-red colour scheme to create an oppressive ambience. We currently have oak-style laminate flooring in the middle surrounded by black and red square carpet tiles. We both agree that the downstairs space is fine, and we should focus on transforming the upstairs into a welcoming and vibrant seating area.

Sharon has picked out a colour scheme and lighting and furnishing options based on what she would do at home, which includes lampshades from Dunelm department store and a cream-coloured emulsion paint from B&Q. I think we need the help of a professional interior designer who specialises in hospitality. That will be more of an investment, but they can create a space that is attractive, modern, and practical for the heavy foot traffic of a coffee shop.

I've invited an interior designer by the name of Andrea to advise us. She specialises in commercial and retail premises and has an impressive portfolio of completed projects on her website, including a bistro, a restaurant and a themed coffee shop.

"These lampshades could probably be recycled in some way," says Andrea. She reaches up and taps one of the pendant-shaped paper lampshades and makes it swing, before gazing at the factory-style fluorescent lighting that goes down the middle of the room. "I'm not sure about the fluorescent lighting, though, unless we replace it completely – and that would be expensive."

"We are cost-conscious," I say.

"I know an upholsterer who could upholster these chairs and the sofas. That will be cheaper than new furnishing." She starts making notes in her notebook.

I like her reuse and recycle approach. Even Sharon seems to be impressed with her initial thoughts.

"For the walls, we can do wooden panelling along the bottom." She positions the side of her hand on the wall. "Up to about one metre high. Natural wood, maybe."

"I would like to just paint it," Sharon says, clearly not quite ready to let go of her own ideas.

We cannot quite settle on a colour scheme, though, and she suggests coming back with her design books and fabric samples. The conversation is going well, and we go on to talk about options for new flooring and wall lighting.

"We want to get started as soon as possible," I conclude. "What are the next steps?"

"I'll come back to you once I talk to my decorators. I know they have a lot of jobs on." She stands up, surveys the room and starts sketching an outline on her book. "How much is your budget?" she asks, still writing in her notebook.

Initially, I had the figure of £10,000 in my mind, but I'm encouraged by her money-saving ideas.

"I'm hoping we could do it for around £5,000 pounds."

She looks up, screws her face and backs away from me. Anyone would think I had forgotten my manners and let off some obnoxious smell.

"Well, OK, take that as a ballpark figure," I say.

"My designs alone will cost between three and four thousand pounds," she says. She puts her notebook down on the table. "My decorators are good, and this will probably need three coats of paint." She points at the red and black wall. "Then we must think about fabrics for the furniture and the flooring."

"We could go up a bit. They're probably some jobs we can do ourselves," I say.

She smiles, almost sympathetically.

"Perhaps the best thing is for you to hold off for six months or so. Build up a proper refurbishment budget. You'll need about twenty-five thousand. Then I can come back, and I'll bring some fabric samples next time."

We say our goodbyes and I take her business card. My five-thousand-pound punt was perhaps a bit naive, but to pay three or four thousand pounds for fabric selection and designs would be indulgent. I would at least expect some paint on the walls for that money. Suddenly, Sharon's idea of a do-it-yourself paint job and buying lampshades from Dunelm and furniture from Ikea takes on a whole new level of attraction. What is more, we have a handyman friend – Paul. We had previously lined him up to help with The Steam Station. He's coming round to do our garden tomorrow, so we'll chat to him then.

We have known Paul for many years. He is a few years older than me and is self-employed. Over the years, he has done carpentry, painting and gardening projects for us, such as decking and wooden planting beds. Everything is done to a high standard and at a reasonable price, and he's also good at reclaiming and reusing old materials. He is an ideas man with a creative mind and can look at space and visualise how it can be transformed into something unique and attractive. He has a strong conviction in his own opinions and is not easily influenced by opposing viewpoints – and this trait carries through on most topics.

We show Paul the images of the upstairs space on the iPad.

"That's wrong for a start." He points to the image. "You want lighter colours."

"That's right, Paul," says Sharon, "I want two neutral colours that tone in, like this." She pulls out her Dulux colour swatch cards. "Grey along the bottom and cream along the top half of the wall."

"I tell you what would look good – wooden panelling along the bottom, about one metre high." He puts his hand against the wall, about the height of his waist. "You can have natural wood or painted panels. Then for the top half, we'll paint it an off-white shade."

"I'd rather we just painted it," says Sharon.

"Let me show you some pictures of a job I did for someone."

He pulls out his phone and starts scrolling through his photo collection. "I did the panelling in their living room, and it looks brilliant."

"No, Paul, listen to me."

This is turning into a normal conversation between Sharon and Paul. I back off and leave them to it. When two people with creative minds and strong personalities start a conversation, there is rarely space for a third person's input. These discussions often have a good outcome, such as the transformation of our dilapidated shed into an outdoor bar with bench seating backing on to bamboo plants.

Sharon and Paul take a trip to the Wickes DIY store, returning an hour later. Sharon comes into my home office to update me. "Right, we are going to do wooden panelling along the bottom." She pulls up a picture on our phone. "Here's what we're going to have. I've ordered enough to cover an area of sixteen metres, and it will be delivered in the next couple of days. So, how about you and Paul fit it next weekend?"

"We may need more than a weekend," I say.

"Paul says he's happy to do a long day. Then once the panelling is done, we'll paint it."

The panelling is delivered on Saturday, and I collect Paul at seven o'clock the following Sunday morning. It is just the two of us, which we are both happy about. "It will give us a chance to have a proper man's conversation," Paul says.

Most of the morning is taken up with re-measuring, marking up, planning and dry fitting, and we make good progress. Paul's a natural talker and while working I'm learning more about betting permutations on horse racing and football. I'm not totally convinced by the logic of his selection methods, but I remember last year he gave me a tip for an each-way bet at Cheltenham and it came in at fourteen to one.

We stop just before twelve o'clock for lunch and coffee.

"What would you like to eat?" I nod towards the cake display. "Carrot cake is nice, Bakewell slice, chocolate brownie – or how about a muffin?" He picks up a blueberry muffin. "If you're doing coffee, I'll have a cappuccino," he says.

"I'll need to go out and buy the coffee," I say.

"Can't you just switch that thing on?" He points to the machine. "I don't mind waiting a bit."

"Trouble is, I don't know how to operate it …"

He walks towards it and looks it over.

". . . and it's on a timer and not programmed to switch on for a Sunday."

I'm not sure how to override it, and even if I did, I've not had the time to learn the start-up process and cleaning routine at the end.

"So, you own a coffee shop, and you don't know how to start up the most important piece of kit in the shop?" He looks at me as though I've just told him I don't know how to use a screwdriver.

"Yeah, I'm embarrassed. But don't worry, I'll pop across to another coffee shop and bring a couple of drinks back."

"OK, thanks. I'll have a cappuccino, two sugars."

I walk across the square, stop outside Costa Coffee and count fourteen customers. I cross the road to Coffee on the Corner – an independent – and I step inside for the first time. It's modern, with climbing indoor plants, solid wooden tables and brown leather sofas. All the tables are occupied. I stand in line for around five minutes, place my order, then I'm handed my coffees after a ten-minute wait. Arden's used to be open on a Sunday – prior to the pandemic. We haven't opened since I've taken over, and when I raise the possibility of seven-day opening, I'm told we don't have enough staff. I've not got involved with the staffing schedule yet and don't know who is available and who is not. Yet previously there was a dedicated team for a Sunday. I walk back and decide that as soon as we finish the upstairs refurbishment, we will open on a Sunday. There is clearly a demand.

I hand Paul his coffee and we both sit on one of the sofas.

"I notice you have soup on the menu," says Paul.

"That's right. Choice of four varieties. We serve it with a toasted ciabatta."

He stirs two sugars into his cappuccino. "Is it homemade?"

"No, we use Knorr catering pouches. One pouch makes one bowl of soup, and it only takes two minutes to warm up in the microwave. It tastes quite good."

He shakes his head. I think I know where this conversation is going.

"Whenever I see soup on a menu in a restaurant or cafe, I always ask, 'Is it homemade?' If it's not, I won't have it."

"I would love to do homemade soup, Paul, but that's another job for someone to do. Then I need to think of wastage."

"I tell you, Steve, I've sent soup back before because they told me it was homemade, and it wasn't. I always make my own soup at home. I remember one time they tried to tell me it was home-made, and I said, 'I want to speak to the chef'."

"What does the missus say when you do that?"

"She hates it. She says I embarrass her. The trouble is, Steve, I can't keep my mouth shut."

Towards the end of the day, I leave Paul to finish his work while I do some shop cleaning. I'm still thinking about the trade I'm missing out on due to being closed on a Sunday. I need to change that. Once we finish the refurbishment work, I'm going to start learning all the shop routines, especially how to operate the espresso machine, as it's painful having to go to a competitor to buy coffees.

We finish around six o'clock, tidy up and leave the place ready for business the next day. I'm enjoying spending the day with Paul. Amongst other things, he is trying to persuade me to take up golf. He often goes on golfing weekends and is convinced I would love it as much as he does. I'm sure I would, but for the time being, all my spare time is being consumed by this place.

We're driving home.

"I noticed you had that mop and bucket out this afternoon, Steve, cleaning the staircase," Paul says.

"Just doing my bit to help. Looks like that was missed from the end-of-day cleaning yesterday."

"That staircase hasn't been cleaned in a long time, Steve. I noticed when I came in. Who does the cleaning?"

"The staff do it. It's one of the end-of-day cleaning tasks."

"You need to get on top of that, mate. You shouldn't be doing the cleaning. It's like buying a dog and barking yourself."

I don't answer, although I know he's right. Staff relations are becoming a bit tense, especially when I start questioning why we have so many people on shift during the quiet periods. I don't really want to get into this conversation with Paul, so I decide to change the subject.

"You know that golfing weekend you were talking about, Paul? Once I get some time back in my life, I'd love to join you. Can you teach me?"

The next stage of refurbishment involves repainting, new flooring and lighting. Sharon and I will tackle the paint job, and we contract with a local firm to install new silver oak-style laminate flooring. We have selected a crisp, light grey paint colour to tone in with the new panelling and help create a naturally light environment. We book ourselves into the nearby Holiday Inn for two nights. When the shop closes on the Monday evening, we start working – the furniture is moved and protected with dust sheets, and we apply the first layer of undercoat. As expected, the hue from the existing red painted walls shines through. Once dry, we apply a second coat, then head back to the hotel. We return at 4 a.m. and apply a layer of Dulux matt emulsion, then clean up and rearrange the upstairs furniture in time for opening. That evening, at closing time, we once again cover the furniture and apply our final layer of paint and the job is done.

The laminate floor installers are aiming to remove the existing flooring and install the laminate boards in one day, and we arrange for them to come in on the Sunday. However, there is a problem with the carpet tiles. They are affixed to the concrete floor with some industrial strength adhesive. "It looks like they had some leftover adhesive and just tipped it over the concrete to get rid of it," says the floor fitter. The carpet squares, rather than simply peeling away, need to be chiselled off, leaving a rough, uneven floor. That takes two days. They make a quick assessment and conclude that we need to do a floor screed to smooth out the concrete before we can lay the laminate boards and that will need twenty-four hours' drying time. The job is eventually finished on the Friday. This is one job I am happy we never attempted ourselves. We then bring in an electrician to change our light fittings and affix four modern pendant lamp shades, purchased from Dunelm. The one last thing I do is to secure some picture hanging rails, which gives us six metres of wall space for the display of artwork.

In a period of four weeks, upstairs has been transformed from a dark and dreary time capsule from yesteryear to a modern, casual-seating hospitality space. "Even the artificial plants look happier," I say to Sharon. We remove the 'No Entry' sign from the bottom of the stairs. Customers and staff responded with statements such as, "Wow" or "love it."

Sharon and I have put in the late nights and early mornings, but in the end, the cost came in at under £10,000. We had to close the upstairs for a week due to the flooring fiasco. There were some noise complaints, but I don't believe we lost much business from that. The original seating remains, but doesn't look so glum now, so we can look to replace that as a phase two project, at some point in the future.

LEARNING THE TRADE

I t's February, 2022. I feel we have come a long way in our first three months of ownership. However, much of what we have accomplished has diverted us away from some of the core responsibilities that are crucial to the running of a successful coffee shop business. Neither Sharon nor I know how to make coffee or do food prep. In fact, we rarely spend time behind the counter or in the kitchen. I'm keeping up with basic financial management, in the sense that the bills are being paid and our bank balance seems to be rising, but I'm still not yet comfortable with our accounting software. This needs to change but our immediate priorities are to become barista-trained and proficient in the kitchen.

Approximately 50% of our revenue comes from coffee, with our three top sellers being latte, Americano and cappuccino. Flat whites, cortados and mochas are also popular. One of the baristas has explained to me that different milk texturing techniques are required for lattes, flat whites and cortados. Other than the style of cup or glass they are served in, they all look the same to me, but I do not doubt there is a discernible difference, and as a coffee shop owner, I feel I ought to be properly educated in this field.

I contact a London-based barista training school, which offers a range of courses, which would take me from beginner to master, covering latte art, brewing methods, sensory evaluation of coffee and many other aspects of the bean-to-cup process. I very much like the idea of attaining this master of coffee accreditation, but after calculating that the necessary training involves a full week in London at a cost of £3,000, I decided that a baby-steps-first approach may be a better use of my time. I then contacted a Birmingham-based coffee house who run barista training sessions — the one Kieran used before starting here — but they were more interested in talking about their house beans and trying to sign us up for a coffee subscription. I decide to call our coffee roasters, Pollards, who are based in Sheffield.

"Hi Mick, Steve from Arden's here."

"How are you doing, mate?"

"Seeing as you ask, let me tell you. I've just had an email from our milkman telling me he's increasing his prices. We had another missed waste collection yesterday because the lorry was 'too full', and I've just spent half an hour explaining to one of the staff that teapots shatter because they are dropped on a hard floor, and not because the dishwasher is running too hot. I could go on, but I think I'm now in need of a sensible conversation."

"Ha ha. Happy to be of service, Steve."

"Can you do barista training for us? I think we just need some dedicated time to learn all the basics of grinding, pulling shots and milk steaming."

"Course we can. If you can come up here, I'll get Tracey to train you. A couple of hours should be enough, after that it's just practice. We can also give you a tour so you can see our roasting operation."

"That sounds perfect."

"Is that lovely wife of yours coming up?"

"Oh yes, Sharon's looking forward to it."

"Okay, I'll warn the team."

We order thirty-two kilogrammes of coffee beans from Pollards weekly: twenty-six kilogrammes of regular blend and six kilogrammes of decaffeinated. We always keep a minimum of seven days' stock on the premises. I did consider switching to a local roaster when I first took over, but our customers enjoy what we serve, we get a good price, and I see no need to change something that is working well. Our house blend consists of South American, Central American and Asian beans; it produces a full-bodied espresso with a strong and slightly sweet taste. The beans are 100% Arabica, which grow at a higher altitude and are considered superior to Robusta beans. It came as a surprise to me to learn that the Arabica variety are lower in caffeine than Robusta.

Kieran, Sharon and I drive to Sheffield and make our way to an industrial estate where Pollards have a unit. Mick greets us and hands us over to Tracey, who is a slim woman of average height, who I would estimate her to be in her mid-forties. She is known within the firm as wonder woman, I guess because she can do every possible job. On the phone, Tracey comes across as friendly and conversational, but one who doesn't suffer fools gladly. On two occasions our coffee order was delivered to our house rather than the shop. Once was a mistake, but when I reported the second instance, her response was along the lines of, "I'm going to throttle them. I told them about that, and they obviously haven't listened to me."

We have built a good relationship with Pollards since starting, but this is the first time we have been to their premises or met them in person. I have already explained that we are new to this business.

"Sometimes we get new coffee shop owners coming to us after their own staff have trained them all wrong," says Tracey. The four of us head into a room where an espresso machine and grinder are set up. "So, who is the barista?" Tracey asks.

"Kieran knows what he's doing but treat me and Sharon as beginners," I say.

"I've got my level 1 and level 2 Barista certifications and I do this in the shop most days," says Kieran.

It takes around thirty minutes for Tracey to explain the bean-to-cup process: the barista grinds the coffee into a portafilter and tamps (compresses) the grounds into an evenly distributed puck, which will ensure the water flows evenly through the ground coffee. Pulling an espresso shot is a two-phase process, involving pre-infusion and extraction. The pre-infusion will saturate the coffee puck with water, which should take between ten and twelve seconds. This is immediately followed by the infusion phase where hot water is forced through the puck under pressure (at least 9 bar). This is when the espresso trickles into the cup. The result should be a black liquid with a foamy crema on top. We serve a double shot as standard (eighteen grammes of coffee) and the full extraction process takes between twenty-three and twenty-eight seconds.

I discover that the extraction time is not a function of the espresso machine but is determined by the coarseness of the grind. When the grind is too coarse the water flows through too quickly, resulting in a coffee that tastes weak or sour. Conversely, when the grind is too fine, water takes longer to pass through, which means bitter compounds are extracted, resulting in an unpleasant aftertaste and sometimes fine particles seep into the coffee. "Imagine pouring water through pebbles (too coarse) then through sand (too fine)," says Tracey. The grinders should be calibrated to give a consistent grind but may need adjusting from time to time. The last stage involves steaming the milk. Creating frothy milk is easy, but texturing milk, to create a smooth microfoam which blends with an espresso shot, is a more nuanced skill and is achieved by aerating the milk with microbubbles. The steam wand should be tilted, and its tip should be touching the surface of the milk; this will create a whirlpool effect which increases its volume as the air is fused with the liquid. The amount of aeration depends on the specific drink being made. A cappuccino will have one third foam; a latte will have a thin layer of foam on top; and a flat white will just have the microfoam. Latte art is a finishing touch. It may not add anything to the taste, but customers love it. On more than one occasion, I've seen people take pictures of their drinks, which I presume they post on social media.

Sharon and I each take turns at making lattes and cappuccinos until we get to an acceptable level. Kieran's already doing this back in the shop and is now in a detailed conversation with Tracey on how to make the perfect mocha.

"Start with half a scoop of chocolate, mixed with espresso. You need to aim to get the right balance of taste between chocolate and coffee. Then, steam the milk as normal," she says.

Kieran makes one, pouring the steamed milk to leave a smooth, brown and cream swirl on top, and has a taste. "Back in the shop, they put a full scoop of chocolate in the milk pitcher, because it's quicker. I'll need to correct them on that one."

Kieran and Tracey continue to chat about the different effects that can be achieved with milk texturing and other best practices, such as never re-steam milk. Sharon is satisfied that she has absorbed enough information. She has a low boredom threshold and is now relaxing on the sofa, drinking tea she made for herself.

As planned, we spent half a day with the roasting team. We

have a tour of the premises and I learn about their range of loose-leaf teas. I may switch to Pollards for tea also, just so we have one less supplier to deal with. I now feel confident that I can jump on the espresso machine, and I will start on Sunday. Kieran has picked up a few tips. Sharon has enjoyed the visit, but says, "I'll leave the barista stuff to you, and I'll stick with doing kitchen food."

"That's a great idea," I say, only slightly disguising my joy.

"I want to start doing salads in the kitchen; we can do one with tuna and a chicken one," says Sharon. "I'll try that tomorrow."

"We'll need to put them on the allergy system before they can go on the menu," says Kieran.

"Yes, that's important," I say.

"And you'll need to train the other kitchen staff on how to make them," says Kieran.

"Come on, that's not difficult," she says.

"It's about consistency – how many tomatoes to use, what dressing to use. If customers get something different each time, they'll complain," says Kieran.

"Don't worry, I'm sure Sarah and I can work it out," says Sharon.

It's a dreary day in late February, and Sharon and I decide to take a trip into London. Due to our exertions with redecoration and training, we missed Valentine's Day, so reward ourselves with a date-day. We bump into some old friends of Sharon's in the station cafe. She hasn't seen them for a while so has a lot to catch up on. The ladies are sitting at a table drinking from takeaway cups. I haven't had my morning coffee yet and, after glancing at what's coming out of the espresso machine and being served to customers, I choose to abstain. The lattes have an excessive amount of foam, as if washing up liquid has been added to the pitcher, and the absence of any crema on the espresso shots tells me they are either using poor-quality beans or the grind is too coarse. I don't think I can trust them to serve anything that's caffeinated and palatable.

We board the delayed train and sit together. Sharon is waxing lyrical about "our new business", enthusing about cappuccinos, paninis and homemade scones. One of the ladies seems unimpressed and says, "£3.10 is quite expensive for a cup of coffee." She then stares into her nearly empty cup, before adding, "A lot of people can't really afford to splash out like that."

This is the first time someone has suggested I'm overcharging. Maybe the acrid aftertaste of the latte she has just consumed is causing her to question the wisdom of buying takeaway coffee. I always welcome the honest voice of the customer, but I have a sensitivity to accusations of over-pricing. I considered my response for a moment before opening my mouth.

"Well, the first thing you have to remember is that fifty-two pence of that is VAT, which goes directly to the government." I pause to let her mentally calculate the net selling price. "The basic ingredients that go into making a latte are relatively cheap, I'll give you that. But remember, a trained barista will make your drink exactly to your liking. Then someone will serve it to you at your table with a wafer biscuit on the side. You relax in a comfortable seat, browse your smartphone or chat with friends. Then, when you leave, someone cleans up after you."

"I'm just saying, people are struggling with the cost of living and the fact is, you can get the same drink for half the price elsewhere, such as McDonald's or Tesco Café."

"Fine. Our customers have other options. There's a Greggs takeaway within five minutes' walk. The fact is, they choose to come to us, pay a bit more and get the quality and great service."

"Well, prices keep rising and this seems like a luxury. Some people can't even pay their electricity bill."

"Don't get me started on the cost of electricity. Everything we sell is either refrigerated, frozen or heated."

I'm trying to mind my manners, even though she's not a customer and probably never will be. I just want to shift her perspective. The rate of inflation is above 6% and many of our costs have increased by more than that, especially the basic items such as bread, milk and meat. Our electricity bill was over £1,500 last month.

We raised most of our prices at the start of the year – as did other coffee shops. A latte increased from £2.90 to £3.10, and most other product increases were what I considered to be reasonable. Before doing this, I costed out the ingredients for our popular beverages and food items, such as the ham and cheddar panini, bacon sandwich, chicken salad ciabatta, then performed some spreadsheet crunching, only to discover that some of our food products were being sold for less than 60% profit margin, and that was before taking wastage into account.

The yardstick I use for product pricing is 75% profit. In other words, if the cost of ingredients is £1.00 then I need to sell the product for £4.00 (before VAT) because most of that profit is needed to cover overheads, such as staffing costs, electricity and rent. I treat cakes differently; they are bought in, and the only preparation required is defrosting. The unit cost of a Bakewell slice is £1.10, but a 75% margin would mean a sale price of £4.40; add on VAT, and the price for the consumer becomes £5.28, which most people would consider unreasonably expensive (even if it is delicious). However, by operating at a 50% margin, we can charge a more reasonable £2.65. Conveniently, our range of beverages yields a higher profit margin – 80% on coffee and 90% on tea, and the fact we sell more than twice as many drinks as cakes means the profit achieved from beverage sales subsidises the lower margin earnings from cakes. The bottom line is that setting product prices is a judgement based on the cost of ingredients and a consideration for what the consumer believes is a reasonable price to pay.

As the 'cost-of-living' crisis starts to bite, much is reported about rising prices for consumers, and a squeeze on household budgeting. I stumble across an online article (from a normally respected media outlet), which has picked up on this theme. The journalist has investigated the price difference between takeaway food purchased from Pret a Manger and the equivalent items made at home. The revelation is that an avocado, olive and tomato baguette, if self-made from ingredients purchased at a supermarket, only costs £2.23, but the equivalent, if purchased at Pret, costs £5.95. It must be a slow news day, and this superficial analysis of the food service business has raised my hackles. I click the 'Respond' button at the foot of the article and make a public comment along the lines of, "Coffee-shops aren't ripping people off and that profit margin is consumed by overheads." I also read through other readers' comments. As suspected, many other postings are critical of the article, summarising it as unnewsworthy and condescending.

I recall some advice from Jon, the previous owner. It was something along the lines of, "Don't undervalue your product." Most customers appreciate what they get for their money and those that don't are probably not worth having as customers. We increased most of our prices at the start of the year. No-one complained and, to my knowledge, we have not lost any customers.

I have found that VAT adds a layer of complexity to product pricing and budgeting in general. It also serves up a cold reality check of the challenges of creating reasonable product prices. After cashing up at the end of a business day, my initial reaction is often one of joy when I print out the revenue receipt; then there is the feeling of despondency as I remind myself that a significant proportion of this revenue must be diverted to the tax man. It feels a bit like a legalised protection racket.

Before entering this industry, I had a basic understanding of VAT; i.e., add 20% to your net product price, as that is the Government's cut. Currently, our VAT rate is a reduced 12.5%, which is an element of support for businesses like ours whose revenues have been impacted by the pandemic. This is only temporary and for product pricing purposes, I work to the standard rate of 20%. Businesses of all types need to add VAT to their goods and services, but for small food service companies, I feel the rules are unnecessarily complicated. For instance, anything consumed on premises is charged VAT at the standard rate, but some cold takeaway foods are zero-rated, e.g. cakes. This means that many products have two prices, one for takeaway the other for eat-in. VAT rules are intricate and any attempt on my part to explain their logic would have a detrimental impact on my mental health. The burden of variable VAT rules means that every time we enter a product into our till system, we need to determine if it has a separate, zero-rated takeaway price.

OUR SOCIABLE COFFEE SHOP

Our steady stream of sociability starts, without exception, with the gentlemen who make up the early morning club at 7.30 a.m. On a Thursday, the traders from the weekly market come in early too. The builders stride in around 8 a.m.: two gentlemen in their early thirties, always dressed as if they are about to recommence renovation work or plastering. Around 8.20 a.m., the school dads arrive. They order their lattes, and their children (who are in the five to seven age range) have babyccinos and sit with their dads, as if practising being grown-ups. And so the happy flow of regulars, occasional patrons and visitors continues. We enjoy good trade from neighbouring shops, such as Elliot the Horticulturist, who comes in for a regular takeaway of four drinks for his staff. The five-to-ten-minute wait time is never a problem as there is always incidental friendly chat and banter with the staff amongst those waiting for their takeaway drinks.

Neil comes into the coffee shop between 8.45 and 9.15 a.m. every morning, always on his own. He is a tall, slim, bearded gentleman, whom I would estimate to be sixty years of age. He orders an Americano and opens the conversation by reeling off a topical news story, sometimes supplementing it with his own opinion. He stays for twenty minutes or so and often strikes up a conversation with other customers. He has a loud, reverberating voice, which sometimes sounds as though he's talking through a megaphone. Neil is a familiar presence in the town of Kenilworth, is often seen walking through the main shopping areas, and always has time for conversation. To my knowledge, he does not have a significant other. This is the gentleman Kieran and I met on our first day when we were sitting outside eating our paninis. He had shuffled by, stopped to look at us, and provided an update on the pandemic and the prospect of another lockdown.

The morning hubbub starts at around 10.40 a.m. The downstairs seating space – which sits thirty-eight people – fills with regular customers and comes alive with a commotion of conversation, the hissing of steam wands, the burr of coffee grinders and the clinking of cups and saucers on the countertop. Staff play tag-team as they greet customers, prepare drinks and deliver orders to tables. The customer demographic includes retirees, mothers with children, local shoppers and those on a work break. Together they make up the multiple friendship groups that congregate and transform this coffee shop into a hive of social connection. The upstairs space normally gets partially filled, but generally, it is more peaceful – one can at least hear the background music.

It is Thursday morning in March, just past 11 a.m., and I'm sitting in a quiet corner upstairs with my laptop open and headset on, enjoying a calm ambience, with nothing more disturbing than the quiet murmur of conversation from two other customers. This affords me the serenity I need to catch up with overdue deadlines from my other job. Two ladies come upstairs and sit down on a leather sofa at a table opposite me; two more ladies join them, and they start repositioning the chairs to make a large circle. One of them looks at me and says,

"I hope you don't mind. There are a few more of us coming up. Our Zumba class has just finished. We won't be offended if you want to move away, I know we can be a bit chatty."

I pull my headphones away from my ears. "That's not a problem, I'm good at working with background noise."

They must be members of Curves, the neighbouring ladies-only gym, which has regular fitness classes. It's located about fifty metres away at the end of the square. I normally donate gift cards for their Christmas raffle as I'm grateful for their business. The noise level does rise a bit though.

"Actually, I'll just move down a bit to give you more space," I say.

Then they come up the stairs in twos and threes. Soon there are twelve of them crammed around two tables, sitting on sofas, tub chairs and pouffes, and it hits my ears. The cacophony of conversation is like the crescendo of a cathedral organ blowing on all its pipes. Their chatter and laughter are reverberating through this entire space, and the staff who are coming up with trays of drinks and food just add to the general kerfuffle. Five minutes ago, I was meditating to the rhythm of my fingertips tapping on my laptop keyboard, now I find myself stunned and overwhelmed. These women are talking as if their life depends on it. This is one hullabaloo I need to escape from.

I grab my coat and move downstairs. It's 11.15 a.m. and the energy of the morning hubbub is at its peak. There are two free tables, but I choose to sit outside just in case more customers arrive and wish to sit inside. The novelty of using my own coffee shop as a workspace wears a bit thin at times like this. It's a cold March morning, and I'm sitting at an outside table with my laptop open and headset on, trying to join an online meeting. I gaze through the ground-to-ceiling windows into the shop. Directly in front of me are Bill, Alex and Stuart: three elderly gentlemen who come every day, sometimes twice a day. I think of them as the three sages. Bill smiles, raises his arm and brushes his hand towards me, as if to say, "Just stay outside out of the way." He often takes the opportunity to heckle me in the shop with lines such as, "It's best if you just leave the running of the shop to the staff, you just get in the way." Michelle is on the floor; she has just served someone with their scone and pot of tea while another customer tries to attract her attention. Beyond them, on another table, a group of mothers with their babies and pre-school children are spread out across a sofa and chairs. One is on her feet, rocking her baby; another holding her coffee cup with one hand and using the other to hold down a child who is wriggling to escape his highchair. Sandwiches, coffees and pots of tea sit on the table. Two toddler children are chewing on their fruit-smoothie pouches. At the counter, there is a small group of people waiting for takeaway drinks.

"Ha! Been pushed out your own shop, have we?"

I look up and see a man and woman I would estimate to be in their seventies, who are smiling at me, and are walking towards the shop entrance. He is using a walking stick.

"Not at all. I'm just enjoying some peace and quiet," I point towards the upstairs. "It's pandemonium upstairs," I say. I vaguely recognise them, but don't know their names. "Don't worry though, there's a couple of empty tables downstairs." I point through the window.

"We come here every Thursday. This is our favourite coffee shop," he says.

"I'm delighted to hear that. Our coffee is first-rate, even though I do say so myself," I say.

"Oh, we just look forward to being served by Michelle," his wife says. "She's so nice and always makes us laugh." They walk slowly to the door and enter.

John, an elderly gentleman who comes in every afternoon, is another regular customer. Sometimes he sits with friends, other times on his own. He will order two Americanos and some food, such as a panini; he may also treat himself to a slice of cake. His second Americano will be prepared and taken to his table after he's finished his food – he doesn't need to ask; the staff all know, and it's a pleasure to serve him. Arden's is like a second home for him, and he always has a caring word for the staff (for example, if someone is off sick, he will ask after them). On the day of his birthday, after he finished his meal, he returned to the counter and handed over a twenty-pound note for the tip jar. He said something along the lines of: "I love coming in here, and as it's my birthday I want to say thank you to the staff."

I've started to reflect on what we have here in Arden's. It's not just a coffee shop. We are part of the town centre's social infrastructure; a place where people connect. For many, it is a form of therapy which enhances their quality of life. I recently watched a TED Talk describing some research that found that having frequent social interactions, even the incidental ones such as a friendly exchange with your barista, is life-enhancing and has been shown to be a significant factor in age longevity.

During my first week here, I recall Michelle telling me, "For some of the regulars, when they come in here, it is the first time that day they've spoken to someone, and that friendly chat at the counter is really important for them." I too enjoy chatting with customers, but I don't really know anything about their background or home life. Michelle does, because they open up to her. I feel quite proud of what we have here as it provides value far greater than just that obtained from coffee and cake. I've inherited this from the previous owner. I feel it is now up to me to nurture this living garden of human connection that so many of our regulars depend upon.

There was some sad news to absorb in the shop one afternoon last month. Word reached us that Neil had collapsed whilst out walking about town. Onlookers rushed to his aid, an ambulance was called, the paramedics took over and he was soon being rushed to hospital. Sadly, he didn't make it, and died. This news was quick to spread as Neil, despite being a solitary figure, was well known and widely loved. The staff were shocked as they had only just spoken to him that morning – as they do every morning when he comes in for his Americano.

Today, a lady in the shop approached the counter and asked if she could speak to the staff. She introduced herself as Neil's sister. She wanted to say thank you to the staff. Apparently, Neil had often talked about Arden's and how nice the staff were, and his daily visit was something he always looked forward to. She wanted to thank the staff who had always treated him so warmly.

A coffee shop should serve as a social hub for all people – young and old. However, every now and again we encounter people we would rather not have.

It's 3 p.m. on Tuesday. It's not been busy, but it has nevertheless been a day of interruptions caused by chatty customers and needy staff. Finally, I'm now settled in the relative calm of the upstairs area, hunched over my laptop and getting on with some honest work. The only customers up here are a middle-aged couple and three youths sitting together. They seem settled and I don't feel any obligation to engage them in conversation. The couple leave and the three boys stay.

I would estimate the boys are around sixteen to eighteen years old. They are slouched on the large sofa and the table is messy with cake crumbs. Within a minute, the noise level from their table becomes intrusive due to their laughing. They are all watching something on a smartphone, and it is quite clear what type of content they are watching (porn) because I hear people having sex. It's not really something that can be mistaken for anything else. I stroll towards them.

"Come on, guys, you can't watch that stuff in here."

I stand over them. One looks up at me, the other two continue watching.

"Can you turn that off please?" I point to the phone. "Otherwise, I'll have to ask you to leave."

They utter something no more comprehensible than an "Uh". But they comply, pause the video and the middle one puts the phone in his pocket. I get back to my laptop and leave them to sulk. They've finished their drinks, so I hope they'll leave. If nothing else, their slovenly appearance makes the place look untidy. Two minutes later, their phone is back on, and the same offensive material is once again audible.

"Excuse me!" I shout.

There's not even a glance in my direction. It's as if I'm invisible. I have already asked them nicely. I close my laptop; my fists involuntarily clench as I stand up and march towards them. I point to the phone.

"Switch that thing off." Maybe it is the anger in my voice or my broad Scottish intonation, but they jolt and look at me. "Now get out of my shop." I point to the top of the staircase.

They pull themselves up, and start walking out, laughing and talking in some incomprehensible version of the English language. I follow and watch as they stomp down the stairs and leave. It's never occurred to me that I might need to eject customers from here. Watching porn in a public coffee shop is socially hostile, but it was their attitude of entitlement and indifference to good manners that breached my anger threshold. I resisted the temptation of giving them a kick to hasten their descent downstairs.

PART 2

MY MOURNFUL
MANAGEMENT METRICS

Juggling my two jobs is an increasing challenge, but I continually remind myself that my regular job comes first as that is the one that pays a wage. I have not yet drawn any income from the coffee shop. Thankfully, I can balance these commitments thanks to my employer's flexible working policy, and long may it continue, as I would never be able to manage my extra-curricular business activities if I had to be in the office every day.

It's April, 2022. I am five months into coffee shop ownership and my estimated seventy-hour work week is split between 25% coffee shop and 75% on my day job. During the waking hours of 5-8 a.m., I find the solitude necessary to focus on coffee shop business administration tasks such as paying invoices, reconciling bank transactions, preparing the monthly payroll and thinking through changes I need to make. Saturdays and Sundays involve going into the shop and being the extra pair of hands for whatever needs doing. This work routine is currently manageable yet is not sustainable. As Sharon commented, "You may be physically capable, but the psychological stress will be your downfall". As with most things in life, she is probably right.

⟜⟩

I am now getting to grips with the bookkeeping and cash flow routines that are so fundamentally important for businesses. All financial transactions go through either my business bank account or my business credit card. Revenue comes through the Point-of-Sale system. Invoices and receipts arrive by email or by paper (delivered with the physical order) and come from suppliers as broad ranging as the milkman (three times a week) and the landlord (every three months). In total, I have forty-five suppliers of goods and services.

Many are simply online transactions, Amazon style, for example Espresso Solutions from whom I buy water filters or Aqua Mundis where I buy the dishwasher detergent. Other suppliers are higher maintenance, such as the food supplier, who delivers twice a week at unpredictable times. Then there are those suppliers who are unreasonably time demanding, such as A+ Hygiene Services, who service our washrooms.

"That lady from A+ Hygiene was on the phone again," says Kieran. "She wants to know when she can come in and meet with you."

"Ah yes, the contract is up for renewal. We just need a renewal price." I say.

"Well, she said she would like to do a site survey and talk you through their different service offerings."

I glance at the customer toilets. "We have two customer toilets and one staff toilet. Why would we need a site survey? We just want a sanitary disposal bin in each, a nappy disposal unit in one and two automated air fresheners. In fact, no different from what we have now! I don't need a meeting about it or a site survey. Why can't she just give me a renewal price?"

"Well, will you follow up with her?"

"Okay, I'll just add that on to my already overcommitted work day."

I am thankful for having feature-rich software to manage all aspects of the business. For example, my till system captures all sales and helps me manage product pricing and stock wastage. I'm now using my accounting system (Xero) for bookkeeping and payroll. There is a data interface between the two and a bank feed into Xero to help me reconcile transactions. I also have a time and attendance system, which allows me to see when each member of staff clocks in and clocks out.

For the first three months of operation, I neglected bookkeeping as I had so much to learn and sort out, including supplier accounts, recruitment, refurbishment and general staffing issues. Nevertheless, I paid all invoices on time and revenue was deposited into the business bank account daily from the card payment provider. However, my neglect of accounting discipline meant that whenever I ran the Xero profit and loss report, I was presented with implausible figures and an inflated VAT bill.

I am now committed to a bookkeeping routine, and, over the last week, I have attempted to reconcile all bank transactions with invoices and receipts. There are four hundred and forty-seven transactions for the first three months, and trying to reconcile them is a job from hell, especially variable direct debits, part-paid invoices and the electricity account, which I must keep in credit for at least one month's worth of electricity.

I can recognise most bank transactions as legitimate expenses, but one anomalous payment jumps out at me. It is £948, taken by

The Osmond Agency in December. There is no invoice or purchase record for this, but I do remember this company. They had called me during my first week, offering a rateable value challenge service, which basically means they will look at how much business rates we pay annually to the local authority. They will perform their own assessment based on location, floor space and the type of services we provide, and if they feel we have been misclassified or are being overcharged, they will issue a challenge with the local authority with the aim of reducing our business rates bill. They claimed to have worked with the previous owner. The deal was, I would pay a "registration fee" of £9.00. If they were successful in reducing the rateable value of our premises, a further fee would be payable. One month later, they emailed me some general information about how my property tax was calculated, which I already had because it is publicly available from the local authority website. At that point they helped themselves to £948 using the payment card details I had previously provided. It has taken me two months to identify this unauthorised transaction. A recent conversation I had with my accountant friend Zoe, is reverberating in my head. "You need to do bank reconciliation every day," she said, her finger pointing directly at me. "People could be stealing money from you." Wise words indeed. This is something I will need to chase up (another task to do).

One routine I have now mastered, with help from Zoe, is payroll. Staff are paid on the last Friday of the month, and I have developed a process which works as follows:

- Download all staff working time and pay rates into a spreadsheet.

- Adjust for sickness days, holidays and overtime.
- Calculate gross pay for each staff member.
- Ensure any changes to employee tax codes are updated in the payroll system.
- Enter the data into the payroll system (Xero)
- Generate the payroll report, which details net pay for employees, tax due to HMRC, pension payments due (employer and staff contribution), sick pay, etc.
- Double-check all payments.
- Schedule payments to the pension provider (for those staff who have enrolled).
- Send out payslips, schedule the necessary bank transfers and reconcile bank transactions with the ledger entry in Xero.

Oftentimes, I find myself researching areas of employment law, for example, two staff members are expecting babies and attend antenatal appointments, which could mean four hours off work. By law, expectant mothers are entitled to full pay to attend antenatal sessions such as this.

Sixteen staff on the books does not sound like much, but the calculations for permanent and temporary (zero-hours) staff are very different and factoring in sick days, holiday days and maternity payments just add to the complexity. When I first started, I used a payroll bureau service. They were good at statutory rules and tax, but they didn't have anything to do with working out gross pay based on hours worked – and that is more than half the workload. I do a lot of this myself now and it probably takes me between ten and sixteen hours in total each month. The days preceding the last Friday of the month are quite stressful as there are so many manual steps in calculating the net amount due to the employee. Once the payroll has processed, I submit the income tax and national insurance owed to the tax authority.

There is an irregularity this month. One of the full-time girls has had an extra tax charge of £560 imposed by HMRC, which I need to deduct from her wages. This will reduce her take-home pay by almost half. I cannot offer her any explanation for this – it may relate to an underpayment in a previous employment or a previous tax year. I know this individual relies on her full-time wage for rent, bills, food and general expenditure and she is a great team member who deserves every penny she earns (which is the minimum legal wage). I make a note to talk to her in the morning, and will offer her a personal advance, which she can pay back gradually.

I am unable to say if the first three months were operationally profitable. From a cash flow perspective, I know more money went out than came in because we have spent just under £10,000 on refurbishment and a few thousand on miscellaneous items, such as new uniforms for staff (although half the staff are still wearing the old uniforms). This was budgeted for as part of the start-up costs and is not a problem, but I have been unable to gauge if the day-to-day operations are profitable and financially sustainable. To do this, I need to be forecasting cash flow and monitoring profit and loss. This now needs to be my priority. It is self-satisfying to see bank balance steadily increasing, but I know some big-ticket payments have yet to be invoiced, such as quarterly rent and the VAT return, and I am unnerved by the certainty of their arrival at some point soon. A famous quote from Michael Dell (founder and chairman of Dell Computers) comes to mind: "We were always focused on our profit and loss statement. But cash flow was not a regularly discussed topic. It was as if we were driving along, watching only the speedometer, when in fact we were running out of gas."

I was chatting to a friend recently, who has been in the restaurant and public house business for many years. We talked about how tough hospitality is, especially as it is labour-intensive. I shared with him that our fully loaded staff costs (i.e., wages including entitlements such as holiday pay, pensions and other entitlements) are around 45% of revenue. He shook his head and said,

"You can't run your business on those staffing costs."

"I know. We're still learning and hope to bring it down."

In truth, the 45% was just my pessimistic guesstimate. I was too embarrassed to say, "I really don't know."

Given that I am time-poor, I decide to give up on attempting to reconcile the first three months' transactions and switch my focus to the most recent two months, as those accounts are in good order (i.e., with all transactions and invoices accounted for). I can now apportion all costs to a monthly period, including services and goods that have been consumed but not yet paid for. Through my accounting system, generating reports like profit and loss and VAT due becomes quite straightforward, and I do this for the previous two months then calculate the key business performance indicators (KPIs) that show the health of the business:

	February	March
Total Takings	£32,774	£35,488
VAT charge	(£3,558)	(£3,842)
Actual Sales Revenue	£29,215	£31,487
Cost of Goods	(£7,996)	(£9,995)

Staffing costs	(£14,954)	(£15,493)
Rent and Rates	(£3,157)	(£3,157)
Electricity and Water	(£1,686)	(£1,494)
All other costs	(£4,030)	(£3,012)
Profit / Loss	**Loss: (£2,609)**	**Loss: (£1,664)**
KEY BUSINESS METRICS		
Number of Trading Days	28	31
Average revenue per day (Takings / after VAT)	£1,170 / £1,043 net	£1,255 / £1,113 net
Cost of Goods % (Target is < 25%)	27.3%	31.7%
Staff costs % (Target is 38%)	51%	49%

I'm proud of the fact that I can generate such an insightful business report. However, the figures aren't pretty. It shows I'm losing in the region of £2,000 a month. I have been feeling positive about this business up until this point, and to receive this report is a bit like opening a special delivery package on my birthday only to find a gift-wrapped bank statement in overdraft.

Zoe has told me that most new businesses are loss-making for the first year, then become profitable through good management. So, I still have optimism. The previous owner started this business from scratch ten years ago and built it up to become a cash-flow-positive operation. The turmoil of the pandemic had an impact on revenues, but government support ensured it remained solvent. I haven't consciously changed much. So, I am left to contemplate how this once-profitable business could work its way into such a calamitous state. Thankfully, this crucial business report pinpoints exactly where the problems lie:

- Cost of goods
- Staff costs

Both ratios are too high, especially staff costs. This problem will be further compounded by two legal changes that are coming into effect this month. Firstly, the rate of VAT is going to increase from 12.5% to 20% (12.5% was a discounted rate introduced to help hospitality businesses during the pandemic). That alone will reduce our net revenue by something in the region of £2,000 per month. Secondly, the national minimum wage is set to increase from £9.00 per hour to £9.50 per hour. This will raise our staff costs further (half of our staff are on the minimum wage, while the more experienced staff are on a higher hourly rate).

To address this problem, I either need to generate more revenue from the same resources or reduce the operating costs. The simplest solution would be to raise prices. I quickly model this on a spreadsheet:

		Potential Price Increase		
	Current	10%	20%	25%
Net Revenue	£31,487	£34,636	£37,784	£39,359
Cost of Goods %	31.74%	28.86%	26.45%	25.39%
Staff Costs %	49.20%	44.73%	41.00%	39.36%
Current prices				
Latte	£3.10	£3.41	£3.72	£3.88
Panini (average)	£5.95	£6.55	£7.14	£7.44
Smoothie	£3.50	£3.85	£4.20	£4.38

I believe in serving quality products at a reasonable price, but a 20% price increase would be far more than what other coffee shops charge (e.g., Costa charge £3.20 for a latte), and customer loyalty can only be tested so far.

To understand the business more, I download all our transactions from our Point-of-Sale system onto a spreadsheet and perform some data mining and spreadsheet analysis.

The breakdown of our sales mix is as follows:

- Coffee: 50%
- Tea: 7%
- Prepared food: 20%
- Cakes: 14%
- Everything else: 9%

Coffee and tea are our highest margin products, but at an average price of £3.10, beverage sales alone are not going to generate the revenue necessary to run a ninety-six-seater coffee shop. The proportion of sales from kitchen food is lower than I expected it to be. This category is important, because the average price point is in the region of £6.00 and most people who buy a kitchen item, such as a panini, will also buy a drink. This is what drives up the average transaction cost (another key metric). If a customer is going to sit in for thirty minutes and get service at the table, we need them to spend more than £3.10. I surmise that if we can sell more kitchen food, without increasing staffing levels, that will surely increase our revenue and bring us into profitability.

I recall my early research, almost a year ago, looking at the Starbucks retail mix, which was broken down as:

- Beverages: 74%
- Food: 22%
- Other: 4%

Clearly, Starbucks focus on the high-margin beverage sales, which is a good strategy for them as it plays to their competitive advantage of having shops in high-traffic locations whilst being able to trade with a recognisable consumer brand. This would not work for us as we could never get the same volume of beverage sales. Therefore, we need to rely on food sales to generate enough revenue to become profitable.

Beverages of all types are high margin and I start to brainstorm how we can build on this further, perhaps with speciality drinks. Bubble tea (a sweet Taiwanese drink with tapioca pearls) may be a valuable addition to our menu. From market research, I know it is growing in popularity, especially amongst young people, and speciality bubble tea shops are appearing in city centres. This could attract a whole new customer segment, even better if they pair their drink with a cake.

Our merchandise display stand is used for the sale of reusable coffee cups, coffee grinders and speciality packaged foods such as fudge and jars of biscuits. This generates very little revenue, probably because people come in for food and drink to consume in the moment and rarely make an impulse purchase of a jar of speciality marmalade. We may sell two reusable coffee cups a week and four or five bags of coffee beans. The most popular retail items are the children's activity bags, which we sell for £1 each (this is our second lowest-cost product after a babyccino drink at fifty pence). However, retail revenue is less than 1%. I have always liked the idea of merchandise as it doesn't take much effort, but it isn't contributing anything to the business. It may be better to repurpose that space to allow for more seats.

The 'cost of goods sold' metric relates to the cost of ingredients that we convert into consumable products. This includes coffee beans, milk, and all food ingredients and those items that are essential for selling the product, such as paper cups and food packaging. This is one area where we have relatively strong negotiating power as there are numerous coffee roasters and food product providers, and we are an attractive customer due to our volume of purchases.

I have a friend who works in procurement, whom I often admire for his ability to achieve discounts beyond what I thought was a bargain price. Whether it's purchasing a car or getting a discount on his restaurant bill after poor service, he is unashamedly relentless in his pursuit of the lowest possible price. He honed this talent in the unforgiving business world of Philadelphia. I've learnt two things from him when it comes to negotiating:

1. Always have an alternative product to bargain with.
2. Never, ever accept the first discounted price offered.

One of our biggest suppliers is Wheeler's, who provide mostly food. Our twice-weekly delivery costs in the region of £1,400.

A competing food product supplier has been courting me for some months. They would love to have our business and they have taken the trouble to produce a preferred price list. This is a gift, as I can draw comparisons with what Wheeler's Foods are charging – not always on the same product, but at least on an equivalent-quality item. I make a call to our account manager at Wheeler's, Amy. She often contacts me to ask if I am happy with their service and tell me about their wonderful promotions, and always finishes the conversation with something along the lines of, "If there is anything I can do for you, just call." Well, there is now.

After routine pleasantries, I get down to business.

"Amy, I've been doing some price comparisons and some of your products are quite a bit more expensive than what I can get elsewhere, for example, your La Boulangerie bread is £2.20 a loaf."

"OK, well it's my job to see that you get the best deal from us. That's why we always do our own price comparisons, and that's our premium bread product."

"Look, I can get a premium loaf of bread from Waitrose for less than that."

"Well, we give you preferential pricing already because you are one of our larger-spending customers, but let me see what I can do for you on this one." I hear her fingers tapping on a keyboard.

"So, I can bring that down for you to… £1.85."

Gosh, that was easy. I have raised confidence.

"I've got quite a few more items to go through. You see, I've also got preferential pricing from another company. Things like muffins and Wiltshire ham are cheaper."

"Can I ask who you are comparing us with?"

"Urban County Foods. Their account manager – Pete – came in to visit us last week. Do you know him? They would love to have our business." Amy is uncharacteristically silent. "By the way, I'm happy with your service, but your pricing is just not competitive, especially with bacon and brie cheese. Can you match these prices?"

"Let's see what I can do for you, Steve."

We go through four or five items, doing a price match on each. It's turning out easier than expected.

"Steve, can I ask if you are prepared to use us as your sole supplier? I'm only asking because I need to check this with my manager, and he will ask that question before agreeing to these discounts."

"Only if you've got the products I need at the best price. By the way, the Urban County rep is going to come back to me this week."

"OK, if you keep your spending at this level, I could go further. Let me try a few things…" I hear her keyboard rattling down the phone. "…right, I can increase your overall discount to 20% across the full range. We normally only do this for very-high-spend customers."

I conclude that phone call with a sense of satisfaction. I'm surprised at how easy that was. I'm sure if Jim – my procurement friend – was on the case, he would have gone further. No matter what discount was offered, he would have harangued and bargained until breaking point. I don't have his personality or perseverance, but I nevertheless feel triumphant with what I have achieved. That is equivalent to an extra £140 a week off our food bill.

Addressing the staff costs ratio is more of a problem, and one that requires a rethink of how we work. The complication is that it involves people, and making change at this level would need someone skilled in hospitality management, and with strong people skills. The business is in a precarious state right now, and if we cut staffing without adjusting other things we do, then customer service and product quality will suffer. The current managers (Kieran included) do not have the experience to make this level of change, although I could coach and guide them. Another option would be to recruit someone with experience of this type of turnaround, but that will drive up staff costs – unless I remove one of the current managers, which I don't feel confident about doing. I decide to double-down on my instructions and push them to optimise the staffing rota to get this ratio down. Ideally, I would like them to start managing the budget.

Back when I was planning to open The Steam Station, I prepared a rudimentary cash flow model, which I believed included all costs of running a business. I did not update that when taking over Arden's, and I should have done, as I am now realising there are several costs I either grossly underestimated or did not think about at all, such as:

- Card-processing fees (1.2% of transaction): £300 a month.
- Waste management: £200 a month.
- Sanitary services: £70 a month.
- Music streaming service and licence to play music: £93 a month.
- Software services: £320 a month.
- Disposable protective gloves:£200 a month.
- Intruder alarm system plus alerting and monitoring: £62 a month.
- Various incidentals, such as water filter every three months, staff training and certifications, routine pest control visits, annual PAT testing of electrical appliances.

Then there is electricity. When I viewed the accounts prior to taking over, charges were in the region of £800 a month. It has now increased to over £1,500 a month. It could have been a lot worse had I not switched to a fixed rate deal. Like all businesses, there's not much I can do about that. I can't think of anything I can switch off.

The bottom line is these unanticipated costs amount to something in the region of £2,000 a month. Most of these, I can probably challenge or negotiate a discount on; others are simply part and parcel of doing business, but some seem unreasonably expensive, such as disposable gloves. I dig into this one a bit and discover that we order ten boxes of 'medical grade' disposable gloves every two weeks. There are one hundred pairs in each box, which means we go through two thousand pairs of gloves a month. Some of the staff are still paranoid about COVID but there are perfectly good hospitality-grade gloves available for half that price. Purchasing over-priced ancillaries is not my biggest problem right now, but something we should sort out.

When I first purchased this business, I imagined it would run like clockwork, and my role would be one of oversight and mucking in as necessary. Right now, it feels as though I've jumped into a tidal river, without any forethought to the perils of underwater currents, and now I'm drifting towards the open sea. I need help. Not just someone who can manage suppliers and finances, but an experienced hospitality manager to transform how we operate.

I can't afford to recruit more people, so this responsibility lies with me.

APRIL

It's been four months since our registration visit from the health and food safety inspector and we are still waiting on the crucial, unannounced follow-up inspection. Today would be a good day for that as Sharon and I are both in the shop, we are fully staffed and there are no issues to deal with. I would like to get this over and done with so we have one less thing to worry about, but some things are just outside of our control.

It is a Monday morning; Sharon and I are sitting upstairs. I dedicate time to my regular job and Sharon busies herself with art. I sit at one end of the long table, fingertips rhythmically tapping my laptop keyboard. A lady customer sits at the opposite end, also working on her laptop. She is here with her French bulldog, Frankie. I've seen her before, and we say hello and chat briefly. Sharon crouches down, pats Frankie on the head and talks in coochy-coo doggy language, before settling down at the table opposite with her sketching pad. The three of us are occupied, the dog is settled, and the background music creates a serene ambience.

A short time after Frankie and her owner leave, Sharon shows me her sketch. It's a pencil drawing of the dog, which she surreptitiously sketched whilst he was staring up at her. His bat-like ears and the cuteness of his face are perfectly captured. We mount it, add it to the art display and name it, *Frankie goes to Arden's*.

Frankie goes to Arden's (pencil drawing by Sharon Williamson)

In recent months, we have formed a good association with Kenilworth Artists – a collective of local artists creating wide-ranging work including paintings, ceramics, prints, cards and calligraphy. We have a permanent gallery of around twenty art pieces on display in the upstairs seating area, which is rotated every couple of months. All artwork is available for purchase, with the proceeds going to the artist. On Tuesday afternoons, Sharon hosts a drop-in art club and on Sunday mornings we have children's art workshops with a different theme each week, such as *Draw a Dinosaur*. The Tuesday afternoon art club is more of a show-and-tell session for Sharon and the local artists. Between two and six of them take over the long table with their sketch pads and watercolours and spend around two hours drawing and chatting. This is normally the quietest time of the week in the shop, so they are often on their own upstairs, except during school holidays, when families and teenagers spread themselves across the remaining tables.

Not only have we created an artists' hub, but the gallery, which consists of landscapes, portraits, and cityscapes, has created curiosity, as evidenced by the number of customers who get out of their seats to view the artwork.

My proposed contribution to the artists' hub is a collection of digital art which I own – more commonly known as Non-Fungible Tokens, or NFTs (these are pieces of digital art, stored on a digital blockchain and uniquely associated with its owner). My original plan was to install some high-definition display screens and publicise the first NFT gallery in the region, which I believed would attract many visitors from the surrounding towns. I am very proud of my collection, which includes a bespectacled dinosaur, an anime-themed warrior, some crypto art 'love' paintings and numerous pieces of digital surrealism. The popularity of NFTs is rising, but Sharon remains sceptical about its suitability for a community coffee shop. So, for the time being, it is a low-priority project. Also, with the escalating cost of electricity, the last thing we need right now is more electrical appliances.

The art clubs are a big investment in time, and on their own don't really generate much additional income. However, what we have created is a friendship community, made up of people with similar interests who want to support the coffee shop, and have become regular patrons. When we started out with our artists theme, the intention was to add a bit of character and community spirit to the shop. It never occurred to me that this could be a good marketing strategy.

Independent coffee shops often engage with hobbyists and community groups in a way the large chain operators cannot. Whether it's an affiliation with cyclists, book clubs, fantasy gamers or local charities, this type of engagement creates a social community and a meeting place, which people will value and depend upon. For us, Arden's has become a meeting place for local artists and a talking point for those who enjoy viewing the exhibits. The exhibits are in the price range £30-£150, but Sharon has also left a collection of prints in a box, which are available for £10 each.

Independents such as ours will always be disadvantaged compared to the large chains such as Starbucks, as those companies will always secure the best locations and will pay the least for their supplies due to their economies of scale. However, independents like ours have the edge when it comes to building customer engagement and friendship, as it will be seen as authentic due to the owner's vested interest in maintaining a thriving community. A large chain, on the other hand, can simply choose to exit a location if things don't work out. Community engagement needs continual nurturing, and the reward is a loyal fanbase who will also be advocates for the shop.

I'm in my home office, getting on with my regular job, and I become distracted by a recognisable chime from my iPad. It's an automated email alert on my coffee shop inbox, which occurs every time a review is posted on our Google Maps business profile. I open it and find we have just received a two-star review. The rating scale goes from one to five, so something has gone badly wrong for a customer to be unhappy enough to give us such a lousy review. I've not been in the shop for a few days, and I start to imagine the worst, such as someone having coffee spilled over their clothes or being served up a black and burnt teacake. The review comment reads as follows:

'Ordered porridge which came lukewarm and uncooked. Staff couldn't have cared less. Felt like a Tesco's cafe rather than an independent with any personality of its own.'

We don't cook porridge; we sell porridge pots, each one containing dried oats and a topping such as jam or honey. You simply add hot water, give it a stir and wait for two minutes; there's not much that can go wrong. As for the customer service, it's not like us to be anything other than courteous, but maybe someone was having a bad day. I log in to our Point-of-Sale website to see when we sold this offending porridge pot. This is not a big seller (we sell about thirty pots a month), so it should be easy to find the exact time it went through the till, then I can check the CCTV to see what went wrong. However, we haven't sold any today. The day before, we sold one pot to a lady (the author of this review comment is a man). I look back over the week but I'm unable to detect this customer on camera. I ask the managers if anyone has complained about their porridge. To their knowledge, no one has. I'm beginning to wonder if this individual visited our shop at all. There are two cafes within one hundred metres of us. Perhaps he got us mixed up with one of those places or maybe this was just a malevolent action from someone with a grievance against us. We don't get many online reviews, which means a single two-star rating will nudge our aggregate rating down. Customer feedback is a gift, and, if we have made a mistake, I will be the first to apologise, but right now, I'm feeling aggrieved that a single person has the freedom to post an unjust public comment like this.

It is Monday morning. I have just counted the cash takings for the previous week (amounting to just less than £1,500) and I now want to pay it in. I stroll into the bank and hand over the cash to the cashier – a chap in his early twenties wearing a perfectly ironed light blue shirt and tie. He starts to count out the bank notes, whilst taking slurps from his Costa Coffee takeaway cup.

"Do you actually enjoy that stuff?" I ask.

"Absolutely," he says, raising the cup as if to say 'cheers.' "I'm not supposed to drink this when I'm at the counter, but my manager lets me because I always fetch him one too."

"Did you know that if you walked one hundred metres down to the other end of the square, you could get a really good quality coffee from Arden's?"

"Well, the trouble is, my bus stops just outside of Costa, and I only have a few minutes before I start work, so Costa is ideal for me."

I consider coming back with a couple of complimentary lattes, but I guess that may be a wasted gesture as I don't suppose he could be persuaded to get an earlier bus just so he could take a five-minute detour to buy up a nicer cup of coffee. This has got me thinking, though, about the different types of people that come to Arden's and the market we are missing out on, such as the customer segment epitomised by this bank teller. We clearly cater well for the retirees and people with time on their hands. We are also popular with young families and people with dogs are welcome. But there is a breed of person who doesn't have time for chat and pleasantries and just wants to grab their coffee and go. I mentally categorise different customer groups. Just as our upstairs gallery attract artists and art lovers alike, we need something that will pull in the grab-and-go customers, such as this bank teller, perhaps an order-ahead facility.

Our Point-of-Sale system has an option to create an online store, which can be used by customers to place their order for pick-up, thus minimising any wait time. In the shop, we could create a dedicated space for collection orders and in effect, have two different sales channels – a digital one for the time-poor, order-ahead people, and a traditional one for those who value the chat and banter with staff – especially when Michelle is serving.

I walk back into the store and mention this idea to the first staff member I see – Carla.

"We need more staff before you do that. It's quite stressy when lots of different orders come in at the same time."

"It might make things easier because the till person doesn't need to put it through. The order will just appear automatically."

"But people will just pick up the wrong drink and I wouldn't know who ordered what. I think it will just confuse things."

I was hoping to just plant the idea in the hope that some enthusiasm would grow, but I know when to give up. I'd have more success trying to grow a coffee tree by emptying the used espresso grounds into a flowerpot. I'll take this idea to Kieran when I next see him; he'll be more responsive, and if there are problematic details with the plan, he'll be sure to pick them up.

I'm reviewing my staff productivity ratios daily. The shop management system – RotaReady – makes it wonderfully easy. At the end of the trading day, the Point-of-Sale system will send the net revenue figure to the RotaReady system. It is RotaReady that has details of how many hours each person has worked; it also contains their hourly rate of pay and takes account of holidays and absence. For each day and each week, it gives me the staff cost ratio, i.e., the staff costs divided by net revenue (which I convert to %). For this business to become profitable, this metric needs to be consistently below 40%, and this can only be achieved by increasing revenue and/or reducing staff costs.

Currently, our weekend staffing costs are running at 35% of net revenue, but our Monday to Friday operation is around 50%. On aggregate, we are loss making, although we are making progress. At weekends, we use a lot of part-time student staff, who are on a significantly lower hourly rate than the older, permanent staff. The difference between an eighteen-year-old and a twenty-three-year-old can be £3-£4 an hour. The students may not be as proficient at making coffee and they need more what-to-do-next type of guidance, but they are generally good on the till and super-efficient at clearing tables and pot-washing.

When looking at revenue, Saturday is always busiest, with till-takings in the region of £1,600, whereas Monday to Friday, they are typically in the range of £900-£1,300. It is the combination of high footfall on Saturday, low-cost weekend resources and the fact that neither Sharon nor I draw any salary for the hours we work in the shop, that weekends are profitable. It's not just the higher staff wages that make us unprofitable during the week, it is the fact that there are phases in a typical weekday when we are low on customers. Yet, the staff are always busy, as in the words of Kieran, "there is always something that needs doing in a coffee shop." However, many of these keeping-busy tasks are not revenue-generating. I direct Kieran to only schedule the staff for the hours they are truly required. The trouble is many staff are on contracted hours and are paid for those hours, whether they are scheduled or not.

From my deliberations, I conclude that we need to be a bit more radical with rota optimisation. The challenge here is the fact that many staff have agreed working patterns, which originate from before I took over; for example, some full-timers work four full days rather than five regular days. Then there are three staff who are not available to work at weekends. When I view our customer flow and revenue generation curve, I see the busiest period is between 11 a.m. and 2 a.m. This also coincides with staff lunch breaks, which means we are always a person down during the busiest time of the day. If I had had this insight four months ago, I would have focussed on recruiting part-time staff who would do a five-hour shift in the middle of the day, rather than promising people three or four full days. Changing working patterns is simple in theory, but switching the existing staff to such a radically different operating model would involve changing much valued working preferences. Forcing through this change would be a bit like trying to manoeuvre a contented bull out of a china shop using a sharp stick. I decide that this is a problem for another day.

FAMINE OR FEAST

I'm sitting downstairs at a window table one late afternoon: slouched over my laptop while sifting through the week's mail, which is littering the floor at my feet. As normal, two staff are behind the counter, another on the floor and one in the back kitchen on cleaning duty. A man and woman stroll in, who I would guess are in their early fifties. They glance at the cake display, then scan the digital menu screens.

"Do you have any paninis or sandwiches?" asks the gentlemen.

"I'm sorry, the kitchen's closed now."

"What food do you have?" asks the woman.

"We have cakes, or we can do toasted tea cakes."

The couple look at each other, murmur something, and walk out.

I slap the side of my head as I watch them stroll towards the other end of the square in the direction of Costa. They were probably hoping for a late lunch and a nice cup of tea in a comfortable environment after an afternoon shopping, and we can't even serve them a sandwich. If there is one thing that is guaranteed to exercise my frustration, it is the sight of potential customers walking out without making a purchase. They may not complain or leave a bad review, but their walking out whilst shaking their heads is a clear indicator of a disappointing customer journey.

I remain focussed on profitability, ideally by generating more revenue, and without the need to increase staff headcount. I sense an opportunity with our prepare-to-order food operation, which requires a dedicated, food-trained, staff member from open until close.

We stop taking food orders one hour before the shop closes, which is the time required for completing the kitchen cleaning schedule; consequently, we cannot serve food after 3 p.m. It is true that demand is considerably less late in the day, but as a hospitality business owner, my key aim is to ensure every customer has a positive experience. If they leave disappointed, they may not return.

Against the advice of my staff, I experiment with a later opening – 5 p.m. instead of 4 p.m. – and thus the kitchen remains open for an extra hour. Customers like this, but food orders are light. On busy days such as Friday and Saturday, we would get three or four food orders in that extra hour, but customer numbers dwindle during the final thirty minutes of the day, so we settle on a 4.30 p.m. closing time.

A second problem, and one common to many hospitality businesses who prepare food at the point of ordering, is our inability to deal with a sudden surge in food orders. Currently, a single panini takes four minutes from order to table. As the volume of orders increases, the wait time creeps up to ten minutes. Surge demand often hits at some indeterminate time window, and this can push the average wait time to thirty minutes! At which point we turn off the menu display screens and stop taking food orders until the kitchen clears the backlog. The staff self-organise and help in the kitchen when needed and set expectations with the customer at the point of order. But the painful fact is that we don't have what I think of as elasticity, i.e., the ability to stretch our capacity to serve a sudden surge in orders. We could employ extra staff, but then they would be unproductive during the non-surge periods and the last thing I need right now is a rising wage bill. This is the curse of a prepare-to-order food operation. It is testament to the quality of our food that some people are prepared to wait for thirty minutes for their order, even though there are other quick-serve cafe options within a five-minute walk. However, many others walk out and those on a short lunch break won't bother coming in at all. I can only conclude that our food-service operation is sub-optimal and not meeting the needs of our customers (and potential customers). In short:

1. No food during the last hour of business.
2. No capacity to deal with surge demand.
3. No grab-and-go food options for customers who are time-poor.

I remind myself that things could have been worse. Nine months ago, we almost opened a coffee shop in a low footfall location – with no possibility of surge demand. That was a close call. At least inefficiency should be fixable; being stuck somewhere with no passing trade is a problem of a whole different magnitude.

I have estimated that if we could speed up our food service, and serve everyone who chooses to come in, we could generate in the region of £120 extra revenue a day, which would mean an extra £3,600 a month and a big step towards profitability. This would be generated from being able to fulfil both surge demand and the needs of grab-and-go customers. I believe my assumptions are reasonable. For instance, between the hours of 12 and 3p.m., we could attract an additional twenty customers spending an average of £6.00 each. Where do these customers come from? Well, many of them walk past our shop on the way to Waitrose to buy a sandwich meal deal. Some of those customers would now have the option of eating in or sitting at one of our outside tables rather than taking food back to their place of work. We could take this one step further with an order-ahead facility.

I recall during our first month here, I was behind the counter. It was around 10 a.m. The shop phone rang, and I answered it,

"Good morning, Arden's, how can I help you?" I say, with a slight sense of pride.

"Hi," says a male voice, "could I order a bacon roll and a cappuccino to take away please? I'll be there in five minutes."

"Sure, I'll put that order through for you now. It should be ready for you when you get in."

"That's great, thanks."

Lucy and Carla looked at me. "You shouldn't have done that," says Carla.

"Really?"

"We don't take phone orders," says Lucy, "because they might not turn up and we would have just wasted food."

"They need to come into the shop and pay for their order before we make it," says Carla, just in case I didn't understand the point Lucy was trying to make.

"Tell you what, if he doesn't turn up, I'll eat his bacon roll," I say.

Five minutes later, a man dressed in jeans, t-shirt and grey bomber jacket walks in. He smiles, looks at me across the counter and nods his head. "Phone order," he says.

We hand over his bacon roll and takeaway cappuccino. He pays by card, thanks the staff and walks out, smiling.

Maybe he was on his way to a job or perhaps it was just ten minutes out of his workday. He could have gone to Greggs, a short walk away, and bought the same combo deal for less than we charge, but he chose to come here.

I feel vulnerable because I don't have hospitality management experience. A fast-service, high-availability food service model is easy to visualise, but confoundedly difficult to implement. What is more, any significant change would involve re-training staff and changing their familiar ways of operating. Up until now, the staff have been training me on food prep. Nevertheless, I have deduced that there are three food-service models:

1. Buy in ready-made meal solutions (e.g. cellophane-wrapped, ready-to-heat paninis).
2. Pre-prepare food on premises and have them ready to heat or just consume.
3. Prepare-to-order (our current model).

Buying ready-made meal solutions is tempting as it removes the food preparation stage, saving staff time and reducing training overheads. This would allow us to shorten the order-to-table timeline and scale up. We wouldn't even need a dedicated kitchen, thus removing a significant amount of labour. Furthermore, our main food supplier has an excellent range of ready-prepared paninis, toasties and sandwiches, individually cellophane wrapped and delivered frozen. All we need to do is defrost what we need for the day, then, at point of order, stick them in the speed oven and serve. We may have to invest in a second speed oven and have both behind the counter (rather than in the kitchen). This appears to be the approach that chain shops such as Costa and Starbucks have implemented to good effect. Of course, they can leverage their competitive advantages. For example, Costa have recently upgraded their food offering through a deal with Marks & Spencer, who supply them pre-packed sandwiches and ready-to-heat items such as sausage rolls. Independents don't have the option of such partnerships. As an independent, we need to differentiate on quality and rely on the fact that there is a significant segment of the market who are prepared to pay a bit more for something tastier than a pre-packaged sandwich. Our ciabattas and paninis rolls are part-baked, and once filled, they are heated in a speed oven for two minutes, which results in a freshly baked taste for the customer, which justifies a slightly higher price.

A compromise between ready-made and prepare-to-order is to make up what we think we can sell each day. If we get this right, it could reduce the order-to-table time by half and so help us fulfil the surge demand. We could also package up premium sandwiches for grab and go customers. The main challenge with this operating model will be minimising food wastage from unsold items. Pret a Manger operate this model and it works for them because they are normally located in very high-footfall locations such as train stations and thus have the sales volume which helps them minimise waste.

We have a staggering fourteen different ciabatta and panini options on our menu. Customers like the choice, but I think we could reduce that to eight without much customer disgruntlement. For instance, the menu presently has both a brie and caramelised onion panini and a goat's cheese and caramelised onion panini. So, we drop the lowest seller and accept the consequence of one or two people complaining because that was their favourite.

Pre-prepared items would also mean that customers would lose the ability to customise their order, e.g., no mayonnaise in the sandwich. I know of some customers who would complain if they couldn't customise but giving them such options is not necessarily good for business. Making changes to customer staples is a precarious pursuit, as I discovered last month, when I attempted to change how we do scones.

Every morning, we make a batch of scones – sixteen sultana scones and eighteen cheese scones – and most get sold by early afternoon. This is a job for the person on kitchen duty and takes approximately forty-five minutes. They are priced at £1.80 and served with two portions of butter (optionally, a small jar of jam for 20p extra).

In the interests of efficiency, I experimented with buying ready-to-bake scone packs – dough delivered frozen from our regular food supplier. This is a much simpler way of producing what is effectively the same product: pop them in the oven for twenty minutes and we have the same result – a delicious, freshly baked scone. This was exciting because I felt I was starting to introduce efficiency without compromising on quality. The staff agreed they tasted just as good as those we make ourselves. However, the customers' reactions were underwhelming. One woman, who was on the point of ordering, pointed to them and said, "They're square." It wasn't a compliment. Some others had a look of disappointment when served, as if they had just been handed a warm, sultana-filled cow pat.

That experiment was unsuccessful because the scones we bake ourselves – irregularly shaped, well-risen, each one unique – carry the essence of homemade authenticity. This experiment taught me that our customers have a subliminal bias for home-baked produce. On reflection, I would like to go further with the homemade approach. It is a differentiator, valued by customers, and it is something that the large chains cannot copy. I already have two ideas I would love to try:

1. Homemade soup of the day
2. Handmade sausage rolls

I have recipes for both. This will immediately improve the quality of our soup, and a premium sausage roll – with freshly baked pastry – is exactly the sort of product that fits in with the essence of an independent coffee shop. This will require some planning and experimentation – equipment, staff training, working space and storage space. I'm also conscious that this is another job for someone to do during an already busy working day. And this is our challenge. I need to reduce staff costs without losing quality. Going all-in for homemade produce increases our workload; ready-made goods and quick service puts us in the same ballpark as Costa and Starbucks – and that's a game we would never win.

Something else we could do is to introduce one or two high-price items on to the menu in the hope that some people would switch from a low-cost option to something better. I have Kieran and the other managers to thank for coming up with the idea of 'pizza subs', which we price at £1 more than their panini counterparts. These use our existing ciabatta bread as a base and the toppings come from our existing food items, i.e., chicken, bacon, mozzarella cheese, and onion. The only extra ingredients we need to buy in for these are pizza sauce and some Italian dried herbs for extra flavour. These are proving popular, especially at weekends. Their creators' preparation is probably more meticulous than is strictly necessary, for instance taking the time to evenly space twelve mozzarella balls on the topping is gilding the lily. However, I let this go because the idea of pizza subs is a good one. They even produced an appealing advertising image for the digital display.

I'm coming to terms with the complexity of food service that is fast and of good quality – it's a circle I haven't yet squared.

MAY

―――――――

I t's Wednesday morning and my day starts with a forty-five-min-
ute exercise session in the park with the military fitness crew.
Eight of us turn-up for a 6.15 a.m. start. Today's circuits
involve shuttle runs, skipping, battle ropes and dumbbell routines. That workout, plus the twenty minutes it takes me to run
to the park and back, causes my body to release the endorphins
I depend on to get through my workday. I have no coffee shop
tasks today, which means I can focus exclusively on my other job
(the one that pays me a salary). I'm thankful that I can still have
work-from-home privileges.

At 10 a.m., my smartphone alerts me to a WhatsApp message
from the *Arden's Management* group:

Lucy: 'There is water leaking from under the
espresso machine.'

Me: 'Oh, dear! How much? Is it coming from the
machine?'

Lucy: 'Don't think so. It's coming from one of the
pipes in the cupboard under the machine.'

Me: 'Are the outflow pipes inserted into the waste
pipe correctly?'

Lucy: 'Let me send you a picture.'

A picture of the storage cupboard under the barista station appears. It shows the plumbing for the counter tap, the espresso machine and the waste liquids. The flexible rubber hoses that carry waste coffee and milk are inserted into a hard plastic drainpipe – as is normal, but something is seriously wrong as there is wastewater overflowing from the pipe, covering the base of the cupboard and spilling onto the floor. It's as if there's a blockage somewhere that's preventing the waste from draining away. I surmise that this is probably a straightforward unblocking a pipe job. Last time we had a blockage, when I wasn't there, it was in the kitchen sink. I called out an emergency plumber, who arrived promptly with a plunger, unblocked it within five minutes and charged me £80. I'm not inclined to spend that money again for something I can easily fix myself.

Me: 'OK, I'm coming through. I'll be an hour or so.'

I drive to Kenilworth, park up and walk into a scene of disruption and disarray. The shop is busy. There are three people behind the counter, one of them with a mop and bucket, soaking up the water from the floor surface, which is still dripping out of the cupboard. Four customers are standing waiting on their takeaway orders and three more customers are in the queue waiting to be served.

"We've stopped pouring coffee and water into the machine, and we're using the sink instead," says Lucy. "It's helping a bit but there's still something wrong."

The customer wait time for drinks is fifteen minutes as the baristas have the extra burden of dashing between sinks while still trying to serve coffees. The counter floor is covered in dirty shoe prints and layers of blue kitchen roll, which are doing an inadequate job of soaking up the spillage. I check inside the cupboard. The mixture of waste coffee, milk and water should flow into the pipe which feeds into a wastewater pump at the back of the cupboard. However, the waste is overflowing out of this down pipe, which means the pump is no longer doing its job. The wastewater pump is a white plastic box with an electrical plug, an inlet pipe and an outlet pipe. It performs the vital job of forcing waste liquid upwards into a vertical waste pipe, which reaches to ceiling hight before a U-bend directs it into the main kitchen drainpipe. Right now, I have no idea if I can even fix the pump or even where to start without adding to the current chaos in the shop, but I do have an idea for alleviating the crisis. I get two plastic buckets and place one in front of the cupboard. I remove the two rubber hoses from the down pipe and position them in the bucket, so all waste now flows in there rather than spilling onto the floor. When the bucket fills, the rubber hoses are swapped over to the other bucket and the one that has just been filled is carried through the kitchen and out the back door, where it is tipped into the street drain. This is the routine we put in place for the rest of the day. It is labour intensive, but it keeps the floor dry and allows the baristas to operate somewhere close to normal.

I make a call to the previous owner for advice, and he tells me there is a spare wastewater pump in the store cupboard. He's had to install one before and says it is 'fairly straightforward'. That's the best news I've had since getting in there today, as I was almost at the point of calling out an emergency plumber.

The staff leave at 5 p.m. as usual. I thank them for doing a brilliant job and their quick thinking and reassure them I'll have it fixed tonight. If not, I'll be back in the morning to help again. I kneel in front of the cupboard, and pull the pump towards me just enough to release the outlet hose. Immediately, the entire contents of an eight-foot wastepipe pour into the cupboard and onto the recently cleaned floor. It's a sludgy mixture of waste coffee and curdled milk. My jeans are soaked, and everything smells, but that is the least of my worries right now. I unbox the new pump and pull out a small instruction booklet, with separate sections in different languages. It looks as though it was written for a plumber rather than a handyman as it talks about pressures and the gravitational force of water. It doesn't come with any electrical plug, so I reuse the one from the old pump. I do my best to follow the diagrams and instructions. If this doesn't work, then I'll have to come back in the morning and do the same bucket-shuffling routine again. Perhaps I should have called a plumber when I first arrived rather than attempting a job I'm not qualified to do.

I assemble the new pump, wedge it into the cupboard, plug it in and the power light comes on – good start. What should happen now is that once the water level in the pump's internal reservoir reaches a certain level (about one litre), it will blast its contents into the vertical waste pipe which feeds into the kitchen drainage system. I pour water down the espresso machine and counter-top drains and allow the pump to fill. There is a short blast – it works. Then it repeats itself every ten seconds – it is as if the waste is dropping back into the pump's reservoir, and it repeatedly pumps it out. This is clearly not right. I switch it off, remove it from the cupboard, dismantle it, compare it to the old one, and discover there is one component I've missed – an internal, hard plastic trap that should be affixed to the reservoir outlet as this is what prevents the wastewater dropping back into the pump. I correct my mistake and reinstall it back in the cupboard. It's now 10 p.m. If it doesn't work this time, then I will call it a night and come back in the morning.

The power light is on, I fill the reservoir and there is a short, sharp blast. I wait and it remains silent. I sense success. I test it repeatedly by filling the waste pipe with water and it functions exactly like the old one. I collapse onto a chair and thank whoever it is that is looking out for me up above. I mop the floor, dry out the cupboard and leave the entire counter areas clean and dry, as they would be on any other day at closing time. I arrive home just after midnight. This is not the day I was expecting to have. I'm too tired to have a shower so I just collapse into bed.

It's Tuesday afternoon and I'm on barista duty. There are enough staff here today, but I need the practice. Sharon is upstairs with the Tuesday art club, who chat a lot and sketch. Kieran is reminding me what milk pitchers to use – the small one for the flat whites and cortados; the larger one for lattes and cappuccinos, and I must not leave milk standing for re-heating. I already know this, but he's probably noticed that I have a habit of deviating from correct methods.

I can see why most staff prefer this role; it's a bit of a creative challenge to texture the milk and pour the perfect drink. I try and get clever by having two or three different drinks on the go simultaneously, the way Lucy and Sarah do, but I mess things up and serve caffeinated to someone who wanted decaf then overheat the skimmed milk, causing it to curdle. The customers kept coming and at one point the display screen was reading, *1 latte, 1 oat milk decaf, 1 flat white single shot, 1 caramel skinny latte, 1 mocha.* Customer wait time was over ten minutes, as I had resorted to making one drink at a time.

Dan, one of the twice-a-day regulars, comes in with his friend.

"Afternoon, Steve. Two lattes please – one regular and one decaf."

"Coming right up, Dan." I release two portafilters from the

machine, knock out the used coffee grounds, dispense fresh grounds, secure them back into the group heads on the machine and press the double-shot button. The espresso extraction takes approximately twenty-five seconds, which gives me a chance to start steaming the milk for both drinks, using the large pitcher. I judge it correctly and pour at an angle into the cup, then attempt to finish it off with some basic latte art. I place both cups on the counter, with a Biscoff wafer biscuit on the saucer. "It's artists' day today, Dan, so that squiggle in the coffee foam is actually a piece of abstract art."

"Bollocks," he says, "you need go back to that fancy barista school."

Every day, at 3 p.m., 'coffee checks' are done. This involves getting out the digital scale and weighing the coffee grounds that are dispensed from the grinder. It should be eighteen grammes – a double shot. Then they record the extraction time, which should be twenty-five seconds. This is performed for both decaffeinated and regular coffee. I've always seen this as an unnecessary task. Effectively, it is just a check that the coarseness of the grind is still correct, and the timing hasn't changed. However, the espresso machine displays the seconds for extraction every time it is used and if it does go outside the twenty-two to twenty-nine second range, then we check to see if the grinder needs adjusting. Similarly, if the shot doesn't look right, i.e., no crema on top, then that also indicates a grinder adjustment problem. I've never known there to be a deviation. Nevertheless, this is one of the items on the list to check every day. These checklists are maintained through an operations management app – Jolt – which runs on the iPad. Alerts are displayed when the task is due, and each one must be signed off to indicate completion.

There are many routine shop tasks which, if overlooked, would be bad for the customer and for the running of the shop. For example, checking there is toilet paper in the dispensers, ensuring there is enough dishwasher detergent. The value of the checklists is that alerts are displayed on the shop iPad if they are not completed to schedule. However, sometimes I feel the staff can be slaves to the checklists.

It's just after 3 p.m., and Carla is mopping the floor behind the counter.

"No point in doing that now, Carla. We don't close for another hour and a half."

"We always start the cleaning jobs now. There's always too much to do at closing time," she says.

I remind myself that I'm not the one who is here every day, and I shouldn't really contradict what the managers have told them. Nevertheless, I suspect time is spent on unnecessary tasks.

If there is one shop routine that frustrates and amuses me simultaneously, it is cake rotation. Every week, we take delivery of multiple boxes of frozen cakes at a cost of approximately £300. These boxes consume two towers of freezer space. The cake journey from freezer to counter display is a meticulous, multi-step process and not all staff have been fully trained on this procedure yet. We normally have around fourteen cakes on display, including gluten free and vegan options and our range includes carrot cake, chocolate brownies, flapjacks, millionaire shortbread and four varieties of muffins. Every day, cakes are removed from the freezer, the required number of slices are separated from the round cake or tray batch using a sharp knife and they are placed in a sealed Tupperware box to defrost. For example, if we decide we need another four slices of coffee and walnut cake, then four slices are separated from the main frozen cake, the box goes back in the freezer and the four slices are placed in a container for defrosting. A label showing defrosting time and use-by date is printed and placed inside each box (four to eight hours defrosting, then a use-by date of four days is common). Once defrosted, the cakes are transferred to the counter display and the use-by label is affixed to the back of the price board so the staff can always see when a cake has reached its expiry date. Oftentimes, two labels must be affixed to the back of the price board, for instance if there is one blueberry muffin on display from the previous day, and we add three newly defrosted ones, then there will have to be two labels showing the two different use-by dates. In this case (and this is important), the staff write a number on each of the printed labels to indicate how many of the older cakes are on display. In this case, '1' would be written to indicate the one muffin closest to the server has that specific expiry date. Cakes that are unsold by their use-by date are consigned to waste, which normally means the staff take them home. I find this routine to be convoluted and time-consuming. I'm sure if we were to make our own cakes and had fewer varieties on display, then the whole process of putting cakes on display would be quicker, and we would recover some much-valued freezer space.

It is 9 a.m., Wednesday morning; there are only four customers in the shop and the same number of staff! Kieran is the manager on duty, Courtney is in the kitchen, finishing off the food preparation and Fiona on the floor, keeping herself busy by folding cutlery inside napkins. Carla walks from the kitchen into the counter area, carrying three boxes of (defrosted) cakes, which she places on the back counter space, then goes back to the kitchen to fetch a fourth box. She pulls on protective gloves, opens the lids and inspects the labels individually. I sneak a glance and notice four slices of coffee and walnut cake, ten muffins of assorted varieties, six brownies and eight vegan chocolate flapjacks. Carla inspects what is already on display.

"Someone's printed off the wrong labels," she says. "Who did the cakes last night?" The cake rotation process is very precious to Carla. She knows every step in the routine and is unforgiving of those who get it wrong.

I wander over, and have a look at the label. "Ah, that looks like the old labels for muffins – without a timestamp – but that's okay because the use by date is still the same – four days," I say.

"We don't know how long they've been out," she says.

"Yes, we do, they were taken out last night," I say. "Just put them out as normal. We'll likely sell them in two days."

"It always gets left to me to sort out."

I conclude that there is not much I can do to pacify her at this point, so I shuffle back to the barista station. In the twenty minutes that pass, I serve four or so customers and leave her to it as she is clearly not in the mood for conversation. She has printed some new labels and writes on some of the existing ones with the felt tip, then she slams the pen on the counter and mutters something about how standards have slipped in this place. She stacks the now empty boxes, picks them up, and walks carefully through to the kitchen just as Fiona walks out. They clash, the boxes tumble to the floor, they simultaneously bend down to pick them up and their heads clash together.

"Argh," they shout. They both put their hands to their foreheads.

I turn my head away and bite my inner cheek. She swears. If her next words are something like, "We don't have enough staff," I fear I'll wet myself.

I find myself in a recruitment cycle once again. Another staff member informs me she is pregnant. That means we have one on maternity leave and two more expecting babies. On a personal level I am very happy for them, but their absence leaves a gap. A new person, however experienced, is going to need time to get up to speed. On the positive side, this may be an opportunity to achieve a bit of efficiency through rota optimisation. I suggest to Kieran and Lucy that they try a new scheduling model whereby only two are on in the morning, five in the afternoon and three for the end of the day, which will reduce our staff headcount by approximately one full-time equivalent.

"We're already down one person and still doing the same work," says Kieran.

"It gets stressful sometimes and we don't know when we're going to get a rush of customers. Then there are deliveries. It's not fair that people end up cutting short their lunch break," says Lucy.

I do now have firsthand experience of serving during the morning hubbub and other surge periods. It does get frantic and my attempts to multi-task while behind the counter normally end in some sort of calamity. I take their point and agree we need another team member – but only for the middle of the day.

I have received a good response from my job advert and make a shortlist, but one candidate stands out and I schedule a zoom interview with her.

Claire lives in Coventry with her family. She drives to

Kenilworth each day to drop off her two children at school then comes back at 3 p.m. to collect them. She is looking for part-time work. According to her CV, she and her husband used to run a café in Coventry. I ask about that.

"We had that until about eight years ago. It was a busy little place, especially in the morning. I mostly did the food, it was all made to order, cooked breakfasts, bacon rolls and sandwiches and baguettes mostly. The government bought the premises and that was the same time we started a family."

"How did you manage to deal with the food orders during busy periods?" I ask.

"You get to know what's going to sell and I tried to keep the options simple. I would also prepare a lot in advance. The cooked breakfasts, bacon rolls and baguettes are fairly straightforward. There was always a lunchtime rush but I'm quite good at multi-tasking in the kitchen."

"What attracts you about Arden's?"

"My kids go to school in Kenilworth, and I've been in there lots of times, with friends and some of the school mums. It looks like a nice place to work. The staff seem to get on well with the customers and I'm quite a sociable person."

"And what hours are you looking for?"

"I would need to finish by 3 p.m. to pick up the children but can start any time after."

"So, something like 10 a.m. until 2.45 p.m.?"

"That would be perfect."

"You said you can't do Saturday because of the children's clubs, how about Sunday?"

"Not a problem. In fact, I would enjoy doing a Sunday because that's the day we go to my in-laws, and that would give me a good excuse to get out of that one."

Our conversation continued and it only got better. She says she may have some ideas to make the kitchen more efficient and her working on a Sunday would be a blessing as Sharon needs to give up working on a Sunday due to a new commitment at her local art gallery. Claire could fill that gap perfectly. As for mid-week, the five hours a day is exactly the type of part-time work we need. I offer her the position.

"Thank you, this is my dream job," she says.

We agree a start date of two weeks' time. I suddenly feel so much more optimistic about the business. If I can continue to recruit like this, we will move into profitability easily.

It's Saturday and I'm in the shop, flitting between counter support, pot wash, table service and generally making myself useful. I make my way upstairs to do some table clearing, and coming downstairs is Frankie – the French bulldog – with the lady we saw last month when Sharon and I were upstairs. She has her two children with her this time. I say hello, stroke Frankie and ask if she's noticed the pencil drawing we have on display.

"Oh yes, we've been in here a few times. I wasn't sure if it was Frankie because I had no idea that lady was drawing him."

"My wife can't stop herself when she sees a cute dog."

"I told you it was Frankie," says the young boy, while pulling at the sleeve of his mum's jumper.

"Would you like it?"

"Really? Are you sure?"

"Of course, let me get it for you." I fetch it from the windowsill and hand it over.

The boy and girl are both holding the picture. "Frankie's famous," the girl says.

"Thank you so much," says the mum. They leave the shop, thrilled at their unexpected gift. I share the happy story with Sharon when I get home that evening.

"Were they OK with me drawing their dog?" she asks.

"They were tickled pink," I say.

JUNE

It's Thursday 2ⁿᵈ June; the schools are on holiday and the
United Kingdom is preparing to celebrate the Queen's
Platinum Jubilee. In Kenilworth, on Friday, there will be a
Jubilee market in Talisman Square and a street party on Warwick
Road. This is the sort of occasion that Kenilworth thrives on.
Many store fronts have royal themed window decorations, Union
Jacks are flying and woolly, royal-themed post box toppers have
appeared. We have decorated the shop with bunting and one of
our regulars has loaned us a large porcelain corgi dog, which we
are proudly displaying.

It's been a busy couple of work weeks for me as I've been
traveling to and from the office in London. I had to focus on my
other job over the last two weeks due to a recently missed dead-
line and the fact I failed to attend a key meeting. I am on holiday
for the next few days, and Sharon and I have booked into a local
hotel so we can dedicate time to the shop. We have advertised a
royal-themed children's art and craft sessions for both Thursday
and Friday mornings.

It's 9 a.m. on Thursday, and families are making their way
upstairs for the workshop. Thirty minutes later, two of the children come downstairs, run up to the counter and ask for Carla so

they can show her their paintings. I'm on the barista station. One of the dads who was upstairs comes to the counter.

"I'll have a latte please and," he points at the tray of pastries, "one of those pastry things," he says.

"A pain aux raisins," I say. "Good choice. They're not long out the oven," I add.

"And can I buy your wife a coffee?"

"She doesn't drink coffee, but I'm sure she'd love a pot of tea," I say.

"A pot of tea then. She's the best childminder I've ever had," he says.

I put it through the till. "We'll bring it up to you as soon as it's ready," I say.

Five minutes later and I take his order upstairs. He is alone, sitting contentedly at the table, gazing across at the children who are congregated around Sharon. Most of them are decorating gold and silver paper crowns with stickers and stamps. Sheets of drawing paper are littered across the long table and on the floor, tubs of glitter have been opened and offcuts of card and coloured paper are scattered around the area. I sense there will have to be a clean-up session afterwards. Their parents are seated at their tables, enjoying their drinks and a period of respite.

There has been a slightly different crowd today, many families and older teenagers. Our takings are just over £1,300, which is good for a Thursday. Looking at the till report, this week has been better than usual thanks to the half-term school holiday, which means families coming in for meals, milkshakes and treats.

We close, finish the end of day cleaning and the staff go home just after 5 p.m. I stay behind as someone is coming in to do electrical testing, specifically a PAT test on all electrical appliances. Every item with an electrical plug is tested, which includes receipt printers, iPads, refrigeration and extension cables. Seventy-five appliances in total – little wonder our electricity bill is so extortionate. He finishes at around 9 p.m. I lock up and head back to the hotel where I meet Sharon for a glass of wine and some food. In our bedroom, I open my laptop as I'm desperate to catch up on recent lost time. I fall asleep around 11 p.m. then awaken at 4 a.m. and get back on my laptop. We have breakfast in the hotel. I've told Kieran we'll be in around 8 a.m.

"I think you need to reduce your workload," says Sharon, "you're not getting enough sleep and you look worn out."

"That's why we're staying over for a couple of nights," I say.

"You're either working in the shop, on your laptop or travelling to work. It looked like you were having a panic attack when you came to bed last night, and that isn't just the caffeine."

"I do feel a bit burnt out. Tell you what, let's do our shift today then take it easy over the weekend."

We wander to the shop. The market stalls are being erected in the square and the traders are adding their jubilee-themed decorations. The shop is busier than usual this morning, but there are four staff on duty and two more are due to come in at 10 a.m. I'm not needed for anything just now.

"Right, there's going to be six of them on today and you don't look well enough to work here today, so let's just go home," Sharon says.

"What about the art workshop?"

"We'll cancel it. It will be fine because I've left all the materials upstairs so children can help themselves."

I go to the counter and say to Kieran, "I don't think we're needed today, so we'll just leave you to it."

"Okay." He doesn't look very happy at that decision.

We drive home and sleep for the remainder of the morning.

It's 3 p.m. I'm still in bed but awake. I pick up my iPad and log in to the shop CCTV system to see how things are going. There is a queue stretching to the front door, and what looks like six or so takeaway customers are standing by the counter. Every table downstairs is occupied. The outside seating appears to be full also. The upstairs is empty, which means they have closed it off. I can see the orders being put through the till, two baristas are at the espresso machine and the floor staff are squeezing through tables and people to deliver food orders and clear used crockery. Thankfully, we have all the most experienced staff on today. This isn't just a momentary surge of customers, it's continuous. Presumably, this is people from the market, which is right on our doorstep.

The shop closes at 4.30 p.m. I log on to our Point-of-Sale system at 5.30 p.m., curious to see what the takings were today. It comes up as a staggering £1,730! Never have we taken so much on a Friday and that is better than most Saturdays. I send a message to the Arden's Management WhatsApp group. There are six members in this group: Myself, Sharon, Kieran, Lucy and two supervisors.

Me: 'I was watching on CCTV this afternoon and noticed how busy it was. I've just seen the takings for the day. Well done, everyone. You've done brilliantly.'

Five minutes passes.

Kieran: 'It's been really tough all day long. None of us had a lunch break. Everyone was rushed off their feet for the whole day.'

Sarah: 'It's not fair to expect people to work like this.'

I decide not to respond. I should probably have anticipated this rush. I'll go in tomorrow to apologise.

Five minutes pass.

Sharon: 'Please don't give Steve a hard time. It was my idea to come home because he's been really stressed recently, and I'm worried about his health. Why don't you all just man up and manage the place?'.

Sarah: 'Man up! I've worked here for years, and no-one has ever told me to man up because we care about this place and always work really hard.'

Lucy: 'It's your coffee shop, what do you expect us to do?'

And now begins the flame war – an exchange of messages of rage. I keep out of it. It continues for an hour; amongst the fervent exchanges is the occasional attempt at reconciliation. It gets to the point where I jump in.

Me: 'All, let's stop the messaging now. I'm coming in tomorrow and Sunday and a couple of days next week. We all want the best for Arden's, so let's just catch up face-to-face next week.'

The messages stop and one person exits herself from the group completely.

I go in the following day for a couple of hours, just to make sure we haven't had a sudden walk-out. The mood seems calm. Over the next week, I catch up with people individually and quench the smouldering fire. Nevertheless, I sense it could quickly reignite at some future point.

It's Sunday and I'm working in the shop. Carla is on barista duty – a role she doesn't want to relinquish, and Sharon is doing food. This will likely be her last Sunday. We have run out of some food items, such as bacon, spring onions and cherry tomatoes, but Sharon improvises well, for example by using Wiltshire ham instead of bacon. She delivers many of the orders herself and explains the changes she has made. There is laughter from the customers.

I'm standing behind the counter with my laptop open. I receive an email from Claire – the lady whom I recruited and is due to start tomorrow. The subject line starts, 'Sorry'. In the body of the email, she informs me that she can no longer take the job and goes on to explain that she has just been offered another job in the care sector, which is something she really wants to do. This is disappointing. She had told me that working in Arden's would be her 'dream job'. We have put her on the rota for four days this week, plus next Sunday. We already have one person on holiday, so the team are going to be short-handed once again. This is bad news. The last thing I want is for the kitchen to close because we don't even have the bare minimum of staff.

I log into the Indeed recruitment portal, and peruse the candidate shortlist I had created two weeks earlier. I need someone who is available to start at short notice and has some relevant experience. Two candidates are top of the list, but they both work in Costa and will have to serve their notice period. One lady jumps out. Her name is Louise, she lives locally, has previously worked in a sandwich shop and more recently in a pub. She is currently out of work and looking for a part-time position. I contact her, explaining that I am looking for someone to start in the next week and if she is interested, could we arrange an interview. She replies within thirty minutes, and we arrange a Zoom interview for the same evening.

I'm not entirely comfortable interviewing someone just because they are available to start immediately. I wonder if there is a reason why they are out of work. Nevertheless, she does have relevant work experience and I remind myself that I should not be influenced by my unconscious bias.

I start the interview on Zoom, and she appears on screen. I would estimate her to be in her late thirties and she appears to be sitting at a desk in a bedroom.

"Thank you for making the time at short notice," I say.

"No worries, I would just be watching telly otherwise," she says.

We exchange the usual pleasantries. She lives with her partner and two children, a teenager and pre-teen, and is looking for a part-time position.

"Could you tell me about your most recent job?" I ask.

"I was working four days a week, afternoons and evening. It was mostly behind the bar, but they went out of business, and the place closed two weeks ago, so I've been looking for a job ever since."

"And you previously worked in a sandwich shop and bakery?" I say.

"That's right, I was a supervisor there."

"Ah, okay. Well, how about you walk me through a typical working day there?"

"I would arrive shortly after nine – after dropping off my little one at school. We would do a stock check to make sure we had all the food we needed for the day and write down anything we were short of. Then we would start making up some baguettes and sandwiches, putting out the cakes, baking off pastries. We'd serve customers and make sandwiches throughout the day so there was always a couple of each type on the counter."

The more we speak, the more comfortable I am feeling. It's as if feeding people and preparing food is just an everyday routine for her.

"How do you deal with an angry customer who has come back to complain about his drink or food or the service?"

"Well, I always listen to what they have to say and try not

to argue. If their drink is cold, I'll just make them another. But sometimes people try it on. I had one person complain about their baguette not having enough filling and they wanted a refund, but they had eaten most of it, so I told them they should have bought it back if they wanted their money back."

We continue talking for twenty minutes or so. She comes across as the sort of person whom, if you met her on a bus, would strike up a conversation and by the time the journey ended, you would have told her all your domestic and work life problems, such was her approachability. She reminds me a bit of Michelle. Someone who would never let you down but would speak out plainly if she felt she were being taken for granted.

She is looking for thirty hours a week and is happy to do Sundays as it would give her a break from her partner and demanding kids. I offer her the position and we agree on Tuesday as a start day. I go to bed that night satisfied that I have averted another crisis week in the shop.

THE HEALTH AND SAFETY INSPECTOR

It's 2 p.m. on Thursday 9th June and I'm back in the shop, sitting upstairs at the long table with my laptop open, headset on and fully engaged in an online work meeting. I hear footsteps from the stairs, and I look over to see someone I instantly recognise – it's Robert, the health and food safety inspector. He is dressed in a blazer, shirt and tie, with his identification badge on a lanyard hanging from his neck. He is carrying a briefcase in one hand. He recognises me too, waves and strides over to where I'm sitting.

"Sorry to butt in, but I've got to deal with something urgent at home. I'll catch up later. Bye." I exit from my online meeting.

Robert places his briefcase on the table and extends his hand. "Good to see you again, Steve," he says.

"I've been wondering when you were going to turn up," I say with a smile. "I was expecting you four months ago."

He laughs. "We've been busy recently and we're also tight on staff."

"I understand."

"How's business?" he asks.

"Challenging at times, especially suppliers. Only the other day, we had a delivery of frozen cakes, and two batches were damaged.

I called them to complain, they put me on hold for fifteen minutes then transferred me to someone in their Customer Happiness Team. I said to them, 'If you care about my happiness, then stop sending me broken brownies and misshapen bakewells.'"

He opens his briefcase and pulls out a notepad and a copy of the letter he sent to me after his first registration visit. He goes on to explain the purpose of his visit.

"Today, I intend to carry out a comprehensive inspection, covering kitchen, servers, outside bin area and toilets. I'll also want to examine your food safety system, the allergen system and have a look at your records and documentation. Has anything changed since my visit?"

"Our menu is still the same, nothing much changed in terms of food service. We have extended our hours and are now open on a Sunday. I've also subscribed to the Nationwide Caterers Associations (NCASS) and I'm using them for staff training, and I've used their templates to update our risk assessments."

"Okay, let's go through these action items from December." He places the letter midway between us, although I'm sure I could have reeled them off from memory:

- Keep hand contact points clean (e.g. freezer doors).
- Clean dust from blades on kitchen fan.
- Remove black tape from freezer door.
- Fix a door handle to cupboard and remove black tape.
- Improve wastebin procedures.
- Identify what action is taken when refrigeration sensors go offline.
- Ensure managers are all able to show historical temperature records.
- Review cleaning procedures for touchscreens
- Ensure all till staff are trained to access allergen

information when a customer asks.

* Ensure ice cream toppings are in the allergen system.
* Produce a health and safety risk assessment for expectant mothers.
* Ensure all necessary training is complete for staff.

I run through the list, explaining how each item has been addressed. He asks about the expectant mother's risk assessment; I open it up on my computer.

"Last time you were here, we had one pregnant lady. She is now on maternity leave, but two other ladies are now expecting," I say. "They've each got a maternity plan and I've gone through the risk assessment with them – avoid heavy lifting and stressful physical activity, such as repeatedly walking up and down stairs. They both work eight-hour days and I'm not sure they'll be able to stay on their feet that long. So, we have a couple of fold-up stools available."

"What about the ice-cream toppings? Are they in the allergy system?"

"I got rid of that self-pasteurising machine. It was too high maintenance. We now have a 'fwip' machine that takes pods — ice cream, sorbet or frozen yogurt. It's much simpler and I got rid of those assorted toppings at the same time."

This was one decision I was happy I made. The new machine is smaller and simpler to use and less effort to maintain. Those toppings, such as rainbow sprinkles, chopped nuts and flavoured syrups, were always an irritation to me as they take up cupboard space and create mess. We're a coffee shop, not an ice cream parlour, and I really couldn't be bothered to put them on our allergen system. Customers now have the option of Oreos or a chocolate flake with their ice cream and this seems to be good enough for children and adults alike.

"Who's working in the kitchen today?" he asks.

"Kieran."

"Can you show me his Level 2 food hygiene certificate?"

I log into the NCASS training portal and pull up Kieran's training records. He is the one person who has completed all possible training courses, including Level 3 – supervising food safety. He is also a trained First Aider. Robert takes pictures of the certificates, presumably as inspection evidence. He then asks to see the latest pest control inspection report. We have a contract with Rentokil, and they visit every three months to check the traps, report on cleanliness and anything else that may attract pests. I know he likes to see these reports because, in his words, "They often act as a second pair of eyes for hygiene standards." I pull up the report, which states: 'The premises are currently clear of pest activity'. Then there is one high-priority recommendation: 'Ensure all hard-to-reach areas are regularly cleaned as food debris is building up by cupboard in the main kitchen'. I'd forgotten about that. He takes a picture of the report. His body language doesn't give anything away. I've been feeling we were doing well until this sentence in this report. I'm thankful I've made an unscheduled visit to the shop today. I'm not sure the managers would have been able to deal with him. They all know an inspection is due, but I've never given them a briefing on what to expect.

The staff downstairs obviously know he's here and I'm hoping they have taken the initiative to perform a rapid clean and have removed the cardboard packaging that had been piling up by the kitchen exit door after the morning's delivery.

We have been talking for around thirty minutes.

"Okay, let's have a look in the kitchen," he says. He shrugs his shoulders into his white coat, pulls his protective hat on and walks towards the staircase without waiting for my consent. He marches into the kitchen, washes his hands in the wash basin (thankfully the soap dispenser hadn't jammed up, as has happened occasionally). The 'Henry Hoover' is sitting under the sink, and he nudges it to the side with his foot. The kitchen area is spotless, and all the waste packaging and rubbish has been removed. They've done well. It looks like they've even polished the door handles. I've never seen it so tidy at this time in the afternoon. I must thank the staff for their foresight. He holds up his smartphone, directs it towards the floor and takes a picture.

Kieran is on food prep and is promptly pulled up and subjected to quick-fire questions.

"What's your policy if a kitchen staff member has sickness or diarrhoea, Kieran?"

"They need to stay off work until they've had no symptoms for forty-eight hours," Kieran replies.

"What detergent do you use for the kitchen surfaces?"

"How do you know if a food order is for someone with allergies?"

The questions come thick and fast. He reminds me of my old high school headmaster, who would stride into a classroom unexpectedly. The class would stand, and he would select someone at random, ask their name, then fire questions at them about the subject we were studying. The rest of us would stare at the floor in fear of being picked on and asked to recite our Catechism. Today, in this coffee shop kitchen, I am the one standing in fear of being questioned. I would struggle to answer those that have just been fired off. Thankfully, Kieran takes his training seriously and diligently puts it into practice, and he couldn't be broken with this interrogation.

Robert shifts his attention to food storage. He looks in every single refrigerator, removes some of the Tupperware containers and checks that each has a label, and the contents are exactly what is stated on that label. It would have been awkward if Wiltshire ham slices were stored in a container labelled as brie cheese. Once again, he is satisfied that we have food storage under control and seems impressed that we have label printers with a touchscreen showing every single food item with use-by dates.

I start to wander through to the counter area, hoping he will follow.

"I'm going to look at your bin storage now. It's outside, isn't it?"

I freeze for a second as I recall what happened during his first visit. "Let me get it," I say.

We walk towards the outside bin store, which hosts a 1,000-litre flip-top bin and a smaller, 240-litre bin. We haven't had a missed bin collection in several weeks, and I pray that today is not the day for Murphy's Law.

I open the door and relax. The floor is clear, and the bin lids securely closed. Panic over. He takes a picture; we lock up and head back inside.

He continues his inspection, including the customer toilets and staff toilet before testing our allergy management process by asking those at the counter how they inform customers about allergens in food if they were to ask. He continues to take photos with his smartphone, and occasionally writes notes in his notepad.

"Okay, I think I've seen what I need to see." He points to the staircase. "Shall we go back upstairs and wrap things up?"

We make our way back to the long table where my laptop sits open.

"I like your food labelling system," he says, "and your management control procedures appear to be satisfactory. However, I have noticed some areas that need to be addressed, for instance lids to the food containers of the salad bar had the remains of old sticky labels on them, the door seals edges to the upright freezer have dropped and the floor covering by the dishwasher has split."

I nod my head in agreement. "We'll get that sorted."

"Next step is, I write up my report and within two weeks you will receive a letter with your official food hygiene rating," he says.

I thank him, we shake hands, and he leaves.

This inspection has been a long time coming. We had done our preparation. I always knew the big areas would be things like temperature monitoring and allergy management – at least he didn't pick up any faults there, yet I'm left with a nagging doubt about the rating we are going to receive. I've been doing some reconnaissance and discovered that every other coffee shop in this locality has a health and safety rating of '5 – Outstanding'. It's clearly a race to the top in this town and that is where we should be. We had a rating of 5 when I took over, so anything less would be an embarrassing indictment for both Arden's and me personally.

I join the staff behind the counter; we all breathe a collective sigh of relief and huddle for a debrief.

"I had to show him how we pull up allergy information on the till," says Michelle.

"Did he find any problems?" asks Lucy.

"There are a few little things he picked on – freezer seal, split in the floor, but I think we're in good shape. We'll find out for sure in a couple of weeks. Thanks everyone, great preparation," I say.

"Did you know he was coming?" asks Sarah.

"I had no idea. I'm glad I was here, but he scared the bejesus out of me when he appeared at the top of the stairs," I say.

"Well, I nearly shit my pants when he walked in and showed me his ID card," says Michelle.

I have learned a lot about food safety requirements over the last six months, such as the types of food contamination that can occur in the kitchen and the potential consequences of allergens. We have colour-coded allergen cards behind the till. When a customer informs us about an allergy, we tick off the allergens on the card, ask the customer to sign, then that card goes into the kitchen with the specific food order written on it. Whoever is on food-prep knows to use different chopping boards and utensils and take all practical precautions to avoid any cross-contamination. This can be quite stressful for the kitchen person. I recall one occasion when Elizabeth, who worked two days a week, had been assigned to food for the first time on her own. She had completed the training and had worked alongside Sarah in the kitchen. On this particular day, she had got through a busy morning without a hitch. Now there was a lunchtime rush – something that always adds a bit of stress to proceedings. Multiple orders were waiting to be prepared, some with special requests. One order had a request for gluten-free bread, then on the next order, there was a notification of allergies. I was helping with table clearing and noticed that wait time for food had crept up to twenty minutes, and some customers were asking where their panini was. I dashed into the kitchen to find Elizabeth crying. Kieran had just come in also – leaving the barista station short. The allergy card was on the work surface, but she couldn't remember what colour chopping board she should be using and all the other precautions she needed to take. Kieran helped and the food was carefully prepared and delivered to the customers thirty minutes after they ordered. I apologised for the wait but assured them we always took good care with allergy management.

Food safety, especially allergen management, add to the complexity of having a food preparation kitchen in a coffee shop. Coffee shops that don't have a kitchen and only deal with pre-packaged, cellophane-wrapped food items have it so easy by comparison.

I often remind myself of the background to Natasha's Law, which has mandated allergen labelling requirements to all takeaway food items that are prepared on premises. This was introduced due to a fifteen-year-old girl with a nut allergy – Natasha Ednan-Laperouse – dying after purchasing and consuming a baguette which, unbeknown to her, had sesame seeds baked into it.

Running a coffee shop is a multi-faceted and complicated business as there are so many responsibilities to keep on top of. Then there is the stress of day-to-day turbulence such as staff absence and equipment failure. However, the worst thing that could possibly happen would be a customer dying due to our mismanagement of allergy requirements.

It's June 16th, 2022. It is one week after our inspection and the letter arrives. It feels like one of those finding-out-your-exam-result moments. There is a bit of preamble, then the news:

The hygiene standards found at the time of the visit mean that a rating score of '5' has been issued. Accordingly, please find attached the Food Hygiene Rating Sticker.

We proudly affix the window sticker to the door. I think we deserve that.

JUST ANOTHER SATURDAY

It's Saturday 2nd July. I arrive in the shop shortly after opening at 7.45 a.m. I have my oat milk latte then jump into the customer toilets to get changed into my running gear, then drive to Leamington Spa for the weekly park run – a five-kilometre race through parkland. I complete the run in a little over twenty-five minutes. At the age of fifty-seven, that gives me an age-grade ranking of 62%, which is respectable, but last year (prior to the coffee shop), I was completing this run in under twenty-three minutes. The fact is that my usual running and fitness routines have been overtaken by coffee shop priorities. I had hoped that by now I would have settled into a better work/life balance. I'm not sure working every Saturday and Sunday achieves that.

Before heading back to the shop, I dash to the cash-and-carry to purchase several items that failed to arrive in the regular Thursday delivery. Missing items aren't unusual, but our supplier seems to have had a meltdown this week. The wrong types of ciabattas were delivered (90-gramme breads rather than the 120-gramme ones), then there were several missing items: such as butter portions, sliced ham and mature cheddar slices. However, we did receive three boxes of Maltesers (each box containing forty packets!) that we didn't order or pay for – but our name and address was on the label, and, according to the driver, "I can't take them back." We have since kept them behind the counter as treats for the staff. The cash-and-carry is still a novel experience for me. It's just like a supermarket except everything is in catering-sized packs or in bulk. I pick up all the missing items and I also add two bottles of Bombay Sapphire gin to take home.

I arrive back in the shop at around 11 a.m., and I'm happy to see all the downstairs seats occupied. I glance at the camera and notice upstairs is almost full and half the outside tables are occupied. The customer demographic is different at weekends: with a mixture of families, shoppers, young people and some midweek regulars all intermingling to form a resonating buzz of chatter and laughter. The team dynamic is also different at the weekend. We have eight staff today, made up of the regular permanents and weekend students aged between seventeen and twenty. The student staff today are Mary, Cathy, Brian and Fiona. They don't have the same ability to self-organise and adapt in the way the midweek team do, but they are operating at a good cadence this morning. Rather than disrupt this fast and trouble-free flow of service, I assign myself to tables and pot-washing duties, which involves taking orders to tables, clearing tables, loading and unloading the dishwasher and ensuring the barista station is re-stocked with all necessary crockery – teapots, milk jugs, and latte, flat white and espresso cups. There have been a few occasions in the past when the baristas have suddenly found themselves without any cups or teapots as they hadn't been cleared from tables or were waiting to be put through the dishwasher. Clearing tables and pot washing is the most basic of duties, but when it's neglected, the knock-on impact is disruption and delay to the essential customer-service tasks.

Today, I notice we are running short of teaspoons and some

customers get thin wooden stirrers instead. It's not the first time this has happened, so I sprint to the local hardware store at the top of the square and purchase some new ones. It's not the first time I've had to do this either and I'm often baffled by why we go through so many. I don't believe the customers are stealing them. The only thing I can imagine is that the staff are carelessly and repeatedly dropping them in the waste bin.

At 12.15 p.m., customer numbers drop to around half capacity. This respite period has come at just the right moment, as wait time for food orders has crept up to twenty minutes, so this will give us a chance to catch up. Staff breaks are also in progress – one at a time, they get twenty minutes to enjoy a free staff lunch. Some of the student staff have formed a huddle by the barista station and are chatting about all the important things going on in their lives. I notice a lot of upstairs tables are cluttered with crockery, similarly with the outside tables.

"A lot of plates and cups to be collected, guys," I say, and I point to the CCTV iPad monitor that gives a view of the upstairs – crockery stacked up on almost every table. They get the message. I go back into the kitchen and take up my position by the sink and dishwasher, which gives me a three-way view: the kitchen, the walkway to the counter, and a direct line of sight down the front of the counter and to the entrance door.

Mary comes into the kitchen with a large washing bowl piled high with crockery, and dumps it down by the sink.

"Are you okay, Mary?" says Courtney, who is walking out of the kitchen prep area carrying two plated food orders for delivery.

"My feet are aching so much. I've been up and down those stairs all morning," says Mary.

"Oh, you poor thing, do you need a hug?" says Courtney.

"Yes, I need a hug." She drops her head as if to acknowledge

Courtney's sympathy. Courtney gives her a hug and they rock from side to side for a couple of seconds.

"Thank you, Courtney, that's better," she says.

I don't think she's been up and down those stairs as much as I have in the last hour and I'm almost forty years older than her. Not that I want a hug – that would be inappropriate.

We stack the dishwasher trays and pass them through to the upright dishwasher, which has a five-minute wash cycle followed by a very hot rinse. This time lets us restock the barista station and kitchen crockery shelves. It's not long before a queue forms at the counter again and a stream of food orders ping through on the kitchen iPad. Courtney has stopped giving out hugs to stressed student staff and is now back at the kitchen prep station hitting out everything from tuna melt paninis to cheesy beans on toast (a recent addition to the menu).

It's 2 p.m. We are back to operating at maximum capacity again, and the customers keep coming. It's one of these surge periods. New customers have been informed that there is a twenty-minute wait for food before they order; then it goes to thirty minutes, at which point we stop taking orders to allow the backlog to clear. One lady sits with her daughter and is prepared to wait. Others do without. I've switched to helping behind the counter and cut up more tray bakes, put out new cakes, blend the smoothies and shakes, and dash in and out to serve orders to customers waiting patiently at their tables. Then, just like the ebb and flow of the tide, customer flow drops, and we fall back to our regular rhythm.

It's 3 p.m., and the staff start some of the end-of-day cleaning routines. We are open until 4.30 p.m., but this is their routine.

One of the students – Cathy – is mopping the same section of the counter floor repeatedly; she seems to be in a dream world. I suspect it has something to do with an aspiring boyfriend who came in to buy a coffee. He also bought her a cake and took the opportunity for a friendly chat. The other girls noticed the shared look of romantic interest, which Cathy denied, although she has been in her own dream world ever since.

It's 3.45 p.m., and we are approximately half-full. Food service has finished now to allow for kitchen cleaning. The remaining customers have drinks and cakes. I'm upstairs clearing tables and sweeping up pieces of food and crumbs on the floor when the happy vibe is abruptly interrupted by the piercing sound of the fire alarm, which jolts everyone. A young child, sitting with his mother, clasps the palms of his hands to his ears. Other customers stand up to leave and I dash downstairs and make a beeline for the kitchen. There is no smoke and no sign of fire, not even burnt toast. I check the smoke detectors and the fire alert points and confirm that the alert has not come from anything in the shop. Two Asian ladies, clutching their ice cream tubs, tiptoe past me towards the exit door. Some customers are already congregating outside; others are on their feet in the shop awaiting instructions from the staff, who in turn look to me.

If there were a genuine fire, it would be quite straightforward – "Everyone out!", and I would grab the fire extinguisher and tackle it. This situation is more ambiguous.

"Okay, folks. this is a false alarm; you don't need to leave the shop!" I shout over the noise – improvising and trying to look reassuring. "We will deactivate the alarm in a minute!" I walk back into the kitchen, thinking this would be the logical place for the fire alarm control system, but I can't find it. Someone from the upstairs gym sticks his head round the door.

"Is your alarm going off too?" he asks.

"Yes, but it wasn't activated by anything here," I say.

"It's going off in every shop along this side of the square," he says.

I make a phone call to the previous owner to ask about the fire alarm system and he tells me that none of us can deactivate it as it's a single, connected system for all adjoining shops. We need to wait for someone from the management company to do that and they are notified automatically. So, we wait, and I step outside and inside repeatedly. The alarm continues for twenty minutes before stopping.

It's 4.30 p.m., and we stop serving. A handful of customers remain in the shop while they finish their drinks and eat their cakes. The closing routine starts – floors are swept and mopped, toilets cleaned, counters wiped down and the till is cashed up. Two staff go upstairs with the floor mop and two are in the kitchen. After five minutes, I realise the *collaboration paradox* is at play once again. That is, put one of the students on a task – like cleaning the upstairs space or loading the dishwasher – and the job gets done quickly and to a good standard. Yet when two of them work together, it takes twice as long. I step into the kitchen; Fiona is standing over the sink with a cleaning cloth in her hand and Brian is standing by the dishwasher holding a pile of plates, but there is little movement of hands because they are deep in conversation. I move Brian into the customer area to wipe down all the tables. I remain in the kitchen and take over plate stacking. Fiona is not inclined to enter into conversation with me.

The student staff, despite their excessive sociability, are great for the shop. They raise the energy levels, learn quickly and their hourly rate of pay is much lower than that of the older permanent staff. For them personally, they make new friends, earn some spending money and, although they may not appreciate this right now, when they attempt to launch themselves into their future careers, this work experience will look good on their job applications. They just need a bit more supervising at times.

~~~

Our takings today are a little over £1,500 and our staff cost ratio is 36% – which makes it a profitable day. Tomorrow will also be a profitable day, but once I do the weekly metrics, I'm expecting the staff costs ratio to be in the region of 45%. We were improving but now we are flatlining. I can't help but wonder how much we could have made today if we had the capacity to deal with the surges in demand and grab-and-go customers – perhaps another two hundred pounds. Hardly a day goes by without my thinking about what we need to do to increase takings at the till, without the need for extra staff, as this is what we need to achieve to become sustainably profitable. Food service is where the opportunity exists. The more expensive pizza subs are proving popular, as are combo meal deals for kids. But this is slow progress on a long run – a bit like crossing the three-mile point in a marathon and realising the finish line is twenty-three miles ahead. I now need to make a step change to how we operate.

Today, we lost trade due to the mid-afternoon surge on food orders which we couldn't fulfil. My ideas of having grab-and-go food – pre-prepared, ready-to-heat paninis and a simplified (smaller) menu, have not materialised into action because it takes a lot of time to put that into place. It involves installing a speed-oven behind the counter and replacing one of the cake displays with a refrigerated food shelf; then there are decisions on what and how much to pre-prepare, whilst minimising waste. This requires experimentation and retraining. I've gone as far as deciding which paninis and ciabattas we can remove from the menu. A couple of the team commented that many customers like the fact that they can make special requests on their food order, and they'll complain if they can no longer do that. I know that is true as I've taken orders such as, "mayonnaise instead of salad dressing, no spring onions and chutney on the side, please." I value every one of our customers, but we can't afford to cater for their contrariness in this way. Changing how we do food and simplifying the menu is a bigger challenge than I originally imagined, and I need some dedicated time to tackle this.

I pull up outside our home. Sharon and I are going out with friends tonight. It's not going to be a late one, because I will be back in the morning for my Sunday shift. I feel exhausted and my feet are aching due to standing or running around all day. I wonder if she'll show sympathy and give me a hug.

It's Monday morning and I've just received an email of complaint from a customer. She says she was in the shop on Saturday, enjoying her coffee with her husband, when the fire alarm went off. She notes that some people left the building while others stayed put. *The staff didn't seem to know what to do and there were a couple of children in the shop who were clearly frightened because it was so loud.* She goes on to remind me about the importance of fire safety and states she was *very concerned by our disorganisation during an alarm* and reminds me this is potentially dangerous.

This is not something I was expecting to receive in my inbox. I sit and stare at the message. Is she really giving me a telling-off? I think some more and compose my reply:

Dear Mrs Interfering Sourpuss from Scunthorpe,

Thank you for your email and your stellar advice on how to improve our fire safety procedures, which I find to be as useful as an ice cream warmer. The alarm did indeed cause panic, especially for that gentleman standing by the service counter, who had just paid for a cappuccino. As for the staff, well I don't suppose any of them have ever heard a fire alarm before. Nevertheless, they are experienced in the application of common sense, and if there had been an actual fire, I'm sure they would have acted with urgency to take pictures and post them on Facebook – I'm always encouraging them to publicise our shop more on social media. Of course, a live fire incident could be a bit unfortunate for customers who, in the absence of good judgement, would remain seated and burn.

With gratitude,
R. Adair.

I deleted this draft before the temptation to click on send became overwhelming; after all I don't really want to jeopardise our hard-earned 5* rating. Nevertheless, the process of drafting this reply has been quite therapeutic.

JULY

It is Tuesday 2ⁿᵈ July and I arrive in the shop at 7.45 a.m. This isn't one of my regular days, but I have a work conference, which is conveniently at Warwick University – four miles away from the shop. The early morning club are sitting at their usual table and three other tables are occupied. The staff seem to be in high spirits this morning, with Carla and Sarah behind the counter, smiling and laughing. They're pointing towards the front windows.

One of the regular customers gets out of his seat, opens the front door and shouts, "Which one did you say you fancy, Carla?" He makes sure everyone can hear. Carla quicky spins round to focus her attention on the espresso machine to conceal her embarrassment.

The two window cleaners are outside. One is reaching towards the first floor with a long, telescopic washing brush, and the other is doing the downstairs window with a handheld rubber cleaning tool, which he is curving across the ground-level windows. They both look about thirty years old, dressed in t-shirts and knee-length cotton shorts. One has tattoos on his arms. Both have the physique and tan that come with a physically active outdoor job in summertime. Cleaning the windows used to be an occasional

Sunday job for me until I decided I should be making better use of my time, so I contracted with these two, whom I had noticed doing other properties in the square. They are happy to have the extra business and the female staff enjoy their regular visits. After thirty minutes or so, the floor-to-ceiling windowpanes are glistening in the morning sunlight, and the two men are each given a drink on the house, which they take away.

At 8.45 a.m., I carry my empty cup and plate into the kitchen, place it on the dishwasher tray and get ready to leave.

"Leaving already, Steve?" asks Sarah.

"I'll be back on Friday, unless there's anything I need to pick up from the cash and carry?"

"Don't think so, the Wheeler's delivery should be here soon."

"Okay, well, bye for now."

"Bye," shout Sarah and Carla together.

It's Friday and we are getting close to the school summer holiday period, but for many older school students, today marks their last exam of the term, which also means their last day at school. It never occurred to me that this could be an opportunity for more business, but it's obvious now as I see happy students wandering through town. Several young people drift in and out of Arden's in search of sustenance. A group of sixth-form girls that I would esti-mate to be seventeen years old come in and order a combination of smoothies, homemade lemonade, salad ciabattas and chocolate brownies and hang out upstairs, awaiting their order. It's a bit like a Saturday afternoon as they sit there chatting, each with a smartphone in their hand or sitting on the table in front of them. They are made-up, happy and clearly feeling good about themselves. A few minutes later, a group of around ten sixth-form boys stream into the shop. They individually order food and drinks.

It's 2.30 p.m., and I hadn't anticipated this flurry of custom, but it is good timing as the lunchtime rush is over; Michelle and Carla are behind the counter, Sarah is on kitchen duty, which is ideal because she is super-fast on food prep and comes into her own when the complexity of multiple orders flow in simultaneously. She hovers between the kitchen and counter, listens to the customer order and before it's even been registered on the till, she's on it; and, like an octopus, her arms reach into all the right cupboards and fridges for the ingredients and she can multitask in a way I never could – panini bread is cut, filled, placed in the oven then under the grill. As two are baking, another two are being prepared.

Ten individual orders come through in quick succession thanks to this group of students, and Sarah goes into autopilot on food prep, oven and grill. The panini dishes are plated and ready for serving four at a time – some with salad and some with crisps on the side, each exactly as requested – then they are dispatched to the impatiently waiting customers upstairs. Calamity Carla is carrying four plates at a time. If something is to go wrong, it will likely be now, but she makes it without any clatter of porcelain on hard floor. Then she returns two minutes later still carrying three of them – untouched.

"I think we've messed up the order. These aren't what the boys ordered." She puts the plates down on the counter and points to them. "There should be two ham and cheddar and one tuna melt. They've just sent these back because that's not what they ordered." She shouts through to the kitchen for Sarah.

Meanwhile, two more customers have come through the door and are browsing the food menu. Typically, just when I was enjoying the prospect of a high-revenue day, sod's law strikes.

Sarah comes out of the kitchen. "Can we check the order again? I'm pretty sure I served everything they asked for," she says.

Michelle is behind the counter and reads out the ten individual orders – one ham and cheddar panini with mayo on the side; another ham and cheddar with mayo instead of salad dressing; one tuna melt, but without onions. The list goes on, and almost every single order has some special request or variation added to it. Once again, I silently curse this 'customise your order thing' we have going on.

"That's exactly what I prepared," says Sarah. "They must have mixed them up themselves."

"Well, three of them have rejected these paninis and said they want what they paid for," says Carla. "What do we do?"

I'm hoping that is not a question for me.

"Right, leave this to me," says Michelle. She comes out from behind the counter, picks up the three panini plates and stamps upstairs. Two minutes later she returns, empty-handed. She places one hand on the counter, palm down; her opposite arm folded at the elbow, with her hand resting on her waist.

"So, I asked each of them what they ordered, then I looked at what they were eating. Guess what? A few of them just started eating the first thing that was placed on the table rather than wait for what they ordered. Anyway, it's sorted now. I don't know if they get away with that nonsense in their own house, but they're not getting away with it here."

I'm not sure exactly what Michelle said to them, but she does have this uncanny knack of putting awkward customers in their place in a way that is more disarming than confrontational. She can easily deal with fickle teenagers, having brought up her own family. She seems to carry this natural authority; if ever a high school needed a Matron with no-nonsense values, then they wouldn't get much better than Michelle.

The value of a coordinated team is evident when a rush of orders hit. That is, until something goes wrong – such as food plates falling on the floor and people sending food orders back for some reason. Anything that disrupts the slick flow of *order, prepare, serve* hits like an unscheduled pitstop, and sometimes it's enough to tip the staff over the edge. But mistakes and mishaps happen! We have what I refer to as a safe-swearing space. It is the staff toilet, which is beyond the rear exit door to the kitchen. It is safe because the staff can go in there and explode with expletives without disrupting the sensitivity of the customer environment. I've seen footprints on the inside of the door.

The week following the fickle teenagers incident, I am in the shop again; we are having a lunchtime rush and I make myself useful by clearing tables, loading and unloading the dishwasher and making sure the baristas have enough latte, flat white and espresso cups to hand and the kitchen enough crockery. Jackie is on food-prep. She is a part-time team member who mostly does the kitchen because she enjoys it and is good at it. Lucy comes back into the kitchen with a chicken salad ciabatta a customer has rejected. It looks fine to me: well-presented, with the chopped cherry tomatoes evenly dressing the side-salad.

"What's wrong with it?" says Jackie.

"The customer wants it to be remade because the top half of

the ciabatta bread slipped off – still on the plate – but a bit of the salad spilled out from the bread onto the plate."

I've never heard Jackie swear before or even get angry. In fact, she is the epitome of easy-going friendliness and always accommodating. But this was enough to trip a fuse. She doesn't feel the need to run to the safe-swearing space, and instead just lets go there and then. The staff in the kitchen aren't exactly profanity-sensitive and are in full sympathy with Jackie due to the unreasonableness of this customer sending back a perfectly good ciabatta during the busiest and most stressful time of day.

The offending chicken salad ciabatta was reassembled to make it look like it had been remade and taken back to the customer. To my knowledge, there were no other alterations made to this food item.

When it comes to advertising to the consumer, social media is probably the most valuable tool at our disposal. We have our own Facebook page, with over six hundred followers, plus Instagram and a website. We also have a listing on social networks, such as Happy Cow, which is a platform for coffee shops and cafes that sell vegan and vegetarian food. We do quite well in that respect, with vegan paninis, non-dairy milk and three vegan cakes on offer.

We use social media for advertising special events and seasonal products, such as Halloween-themed drinks and cream teas. However, this channel is somewhat limiting as it only reaches those who follow us, and they are likely to be existing customers who would come into the shop anyway. It doesn't reach potential new customers. There is a much larger community Facebook group called *Kenilworth Vibes*, which has almost two and a half thousand followers. However, this is exclusively for community-related events and businesses are not permitted to use it for advertising. Then one day, someone posted the following:

I hope this is okay to post, I just wanted to say a big thank you to Ardens
I visited earlier to have a quick coffee and snack, i had walked to the library and wanted a sit down and some shade before heading home, my 2 year old had other plans 🫠
I was close to leaving my coffee and going straight home as my boy's tantrum was getting out of hand. I'd forgotten to get him a babychino (like the fruit pouch and kids activity set weren't enough! 😅) But I didn't have the 50p in cash and the min card transaction is £1, I was contemplating buying something else to make up the money, but the lady was so so so kind, so told me not to worry and she would sort it out. She got him his oat babychino, plus a lotus biscuit and some raisins! He calmed right down and acted like nothing had even happened!
I know the lady said it wasn't a big deal and she's been in my shoes, but it was a big deal for me. My boy is very headstrong and his tantrums are sometimes overwhelming, so to have someone really notice and help out is just very kind and I really appreciated it.

(Sorry I don't know the ladies name, she is always in the shop, she has long dark hair)

Also, the coffee is lovely as was the banana and choc loaf. Arden's is a lovely place they always have plant milk and some vegan cake and sandwich options which is really great 🌱😋

(Also thanks to the lady customer who came over and said how patient I had been with my boy...means a lot to me, as I certainly don't feel patient!)

What a fantastic place Kenilworth is to live 💜

👍😍❤️ 474   67 comments

Wow! This is publicity that money cannot buy – a simple post of gratitude mentioning the friendliness of our staff, the quality of our products, and our range of vegan options. It's visible to over two thousand Kenilworth residents, and, most importantly, it has authenticity. I find this truly heartwarming and feel very proud. However, I am surprised to see so many comments and reactions – four hundred and seventy-four icon reactions and sixty-seven comments seems like an overreaction to something that isn't in the least bit controversial. So, I read through the comments in case there is an underlying sub-story I've not picked up on:

They're all lovely but Michelle goes beyond good service and is just so friendly and welcoming. Love Ardens 💜💜💜

1y   Like   Reply

Awwww we absolutely love Arden's and all the lovely people that work there! You're an amazing mumma

1y   Like   Reply
↳ View 1 reply

Ardens is a fab place. If it was Michelle then she is lovely nothing is ever too much trouble for her. Fantastic little team. Well done Ardens.

1y   Like   Reply

It only got better, with others expressing the same sentiment. Then, someone felt the need to post this:

Well to be honest rewarding tantrums is gonna cause more tantrums. I like the sentiment of her doing something nice but perhaps change parenting styles and you won't have horrendous tantrums. My son is 4 and never ever has he thrown a public tantrum he has been taught a better way to express himself. I'm so angry that society accepts and rewards such poor behaviour isn't of doing better at being a parent and role model. Well done Arden's of offering a great customer experience but they really shouldn't have too, we need to press reset on modern parenting it's clearly not working!

1y   Like   Reply   Edited

Author   Top Contributor
Wow...I'm glad you haven't had to deal with tantrums in public, would you like a gold sticker?
Why would you assume you know my parenting styles, or feel you need to give me condescending advice. Next time I'll be sure to leave my coffee, cake and walk out of the cafe, drag my child screaming and leave him crying...or not.

1y   Like   Reply   2

yes I would love a gold sticker as clearly I am the minority and doing it better than most haha!! I'm glad you acknowledge what you should have done it's just a shame you didn't actually do it as your child may learn that what you say means something if you can drag yourself away from coffee and cafe for the greater good and to ensure your child understands actions have repercussions.

1y   Like   Reply   3

you are a great mum , completely ignore stupid comments by certain people   has melt downs too as do most 2 year olds as they are still learning to control and express their feelings when they get overwhelmed by them . Keep on doing the amazing job you are already doing xxx

1y   Like   Reply   3

The comments continue, and what followed was what I believe is colloquially known as a 'social media shitstorm.' This is not a thread I am going to contribute to in anyway. Suffice it to say, this is one I will remember for a long time to come.

It is fair to say that our approach to marketing has been ad hoc. We have been successful in our association with the art lover community, and that is something I am proud of, but there are clearly some market segments we are missing out on, i.e., the pick-up-and-go people. That is something I intend to work on. In the meantime, I remain grateful for the power of social media.

MY SUNDAY SHIFT

Sunday is my favourite day in the coffee shop because I'm in charge. I don't have to pander to Kieran's pedantry or stick to the regimented opening and closing routines. I'm now competent in making the full range of coffees, food prep and pretty much all operational tasks. Our E71 espresso machine is an intimidating piece of kit, and is the workhorse of this enterprise, but, once started up, its operation is straightforward.

We open at 9.30 a.m. on a Sunday. I arrive at 8.30 a.m., start up the oven and get the frozen pastries out ready to be baked off. The staff are due in at 9 a.m. I have a regular Sunday crew consisting of three sixth-form students – Nia, Grace and Priya – and Louise. I am so grateful to have discovered Louise. It was only due to Claire dropping out of the job at the last minute that caused me to interview and recruit her. She enjoys working on food-prep and my intention is to make her the Sunday manager in the future. She has worked in hospitality for years, can easily adapt to complications that arise in the day and has a no-nonsense communication style and makes sure tasks get done properly – whether it is cleaning or preparing food. This has been the regular Sunday crew for over a month and it's a team that has gelled and work well together.

Louise arrives first, then Priya, with Grace just behind. Two minutes later Nia marches in, munching her way through a packet of Percy Pig jellied sweets. I nod towards the packet.

"You shouldn't be eating those in the morning, they will give you a sugar rush followed by an energy dip and a bad mood."

"You've told me that before," she says without looking at me, then disappears into the kitchen, signalling the end of that conversation and the start of a new one with Louise. Sounds like she's having boyfriend issues again. I can't help but pick up snippets of the conversation.

"Sometimes they're just not worth it," says Louise. This candour, I suspect, has come from life experience, and that is now making her a bit of an agony aunt to the girls.

Nia comes back out of the kitchen with Priya and Grace, and they work through the pre-opening checklist on the iPad – check tea caddies and syrup dispensers, check the use-by dates of all cakes on display, inspect customer toilets, turn on the dishwasher. Nia is on coffee duty today and is running three test shots and checking the extraction times. I check the cash float for the day and put out some fresh cakes.

Sunday is a good day to try out new product ideas, and last night I made a lemon drizzle cake, baked in a loaf tin – one of my tried-and-tested recipes. It has that uneven, light-brown, home-made look and a crispy iced topping formed from the freshly squeezed lemon juice and icing sugar mixture. I had pierced the sponge before pouring the icing over it to allow the sweet icing to fuse into the tangy, lemon sponge. This is one of my signature cakes and this is the first time I've brought one into the coffee shop. Not that we have a problem with our existing cakes – they are popular and include gluten-free and vegan options – though they are delivered frozen every week and are subject to our ridiculous cake rotation procedure. I love the idea of having at least some cakes we can call homemade. Kieran has told me that we shouldn't be selling cakes that are not made on a premises that isn't registered with the health and food safety authorities. That's a fair point; but this is just a trial, and I have been careful to put all ingredients and allergy information on our Nutritics allergy system and Point-of-Sale system. I proudly label the cake, *Homemade Lemon Drizzle Cake*.

Four Eastern European gentlemen – regulars – come into the shop.

"Are you open?" they ask with hesitation.

"Not officially, but no worries, what can I get you?" I abandon the cake display and tap the Point-of-Sale screen, which takes a moment to come alive.

"Two double espressos, a single espresso, a flat white and a bottle of still water, please."

I put the order through. The coffee orders appear on the iPad on the barista station. Nia grabs the portafilters and gets their coffees going.

"Do you have any croissants today?" he asks, hopefully.

"They're still in the oven, be about five or ten minutes."

"That's okay. Can we have four almond croissants?"

"Sure. I'll have them brought over to you when they're ready."

It's only 9.20 a.m.; we haven't finished the pre-opening tasks yet, but I'm not in the business of turning away customers.

The front door swings open again.

"Morning, Steve."

It's Kirk the personal trainer from the upstairs gym and his buddy.

"Top of the morning to you, gentlemen, what are you having?" I ask.

"Two lattes, and two of your delicious toasted teacakes, my good man."

"I'll get my best barista on the job straight away." I turn to Nia, but she's already removed the milk from the fridge.

Louise appears at the counter front.

"Perfect timing, Louise. Can you do the teacakes for Kirk?"

She looks at her watch, looks at me, then turns to the customers. "Would you like them with honey or jam?"

Kirk and I are of a similar age, and we often talk about exercise, although my fitness regime is not quite at his standard. He's a seven-day-a-week fitness freak who does Ironman events.

"I've started a new strength-building challenge," I boast.

"What's that then?"

"One hundred press-ups a day, in sets of twenty-five."

"Well done. Are you mixing up the technique?"

"What do you mean?"

"Altering your hand positioning to work different muscle sets." He extends his arms, palms facing me in a diamond shape. "Close-grip press will activate your triceps. Wide-grip will work your pecs and lats. It will give you better muscle definition across shoulders, chest and arms."

"Thanks for the tip. I'll give it a go."

He gives me the thumbs up and sits down.

Every time I talk to Kirk, I get a free micro-coaching session. I remind myself to come up with some high-protein drinks for the menu, which should be as simple as adding protein powder to the existing milkshake recipes. I could then invent some inspiring names, such as Power Punch. This might attract more customers from the gym above or some ladies from Curves fitness studio just along the square from us.

Nia makes the lattes with her trademark latte art and places them on the counter. She picks up the iPad.

"The opening checklist hasn't been signed off," she says.

"Don't worry, I've done most of it."

"What about the dishwasher?"

"Nothing needs washing just yet, but I'll get it in a minute."

"Kieran says we need to finish the opening checklist before opening."

I turn the digital menu screens on. "I tell you what, why don't you stay on barista duty today, perhaps train up Grace and Priya if you get a chance." That makes her smile. I don't know what Nia's intentions are after finishing school next year, but if she decides not to go to university, I would love to train her up as a manager. I think she would be a great leader.

Talisman Square is coming to life. A young couple with a dog and a pushchair, a dad with a young child on his shoulders, and some shoppers glancing through our window as they walk towards Waitrose. Our floor-to ceiling-windows are great for people-watching and they give me a good view of Costa Coffee. It's about one hundred metres away, where the square joins Warwick Road. I see people walking in and others coming out with takeaway cups. They have the best location as they get people from the square and those walking along the busy main road. I expect they will have more customers than us right now and fewer staff.

Louise comes out from the kitchen, and points to the Tupperware box on the refrigerator top. "Shall I put the rest of these chocolate brownies out, Steve?"

"Thanks, Louise. I'd forgotten about them."

A young couple I don't recognise walk in and Grace takes their order. I overhear an unusual coffee request. The couple sit down, Grace and Nia have a conversation, then call me over.

"That last customer has asked for a dry cappuccino," Nia says. "That doesn't make sense, should I just make it as normal?"

"Well, it's not on the menu, but in this wonderful world of

artisan coffee, such a thing does exist," I say. "It's just a cappuccino with more froth than usual," I picked up the milk pitcher and put it under the steam wand. "In fact, it's almost all foam. Let me show you."

She grabs the pitcher off me.

"I know how to do it," she says.

She makes the drink. Priya delivers it to the customer, who thanks her and takes a sip.

"That's perfect," he says.

Sunday is a good training day for new staff. Priya has been with us for about one month. She is an enthusiastic individual, customer-friendly and a team player who will take the initiative and step in to help others when it gets busy. One customer comes to the counter and orders a cappuccino, a pot of Earl Grey tea and two cakes. Nia is already working through the previous coffee orders, so Priya jumps in. She picks out a teapot, spoons in the exact quantity of loose-leaf tea and fills it with hot water, then fills a milk jug and places it on the tray alongside the teapot. She then skips from behind the counter to the serving area, picks up the tray and takes it to the customer's table with all the cheerfulness of a schoolchild doing a show-and-tell. One minute later, the customer comes back to the counter to ask if he could have a cup so he could drink his tea.

I never chide or laugh at anyone for innocent mistakes. I cannot, as I have made my own blunders. I recall, during my first month, boasting to the staff about my cake-baking abilities and offering to make the scones one morning. They came out of the oven looking as they should – well-risen, of slightly different sizes and smelling delicious. We sold six before I tasted one and realised it was too dry. That's when it had dawned on me: I had forgotten to add butter to the flour mix.

Then there was the Saturday afternoon when I jumped in to help with the smoothies and milkshakes during a rush period. We have two high-performance blenders which can pulverise iced cubes and frozen fruit. I poured ingredients into each, closed the sound enclosures and switched them on simultaneously – forgetting to put the lid on the jugs. I spent the next ten minutes cleaning up the mess, and the customers had a longer-than-expected wait for their shakes. As I'm the boss, no one thinks of teaching me how to do some of the basics. I either need to explicitly ask or learn by trial and error. Most of the time, it's the latter.

Grace has been working for us slightly longer than Priya. She's great on the till but doesn't quite have the necessary speed. She carefully considers each order before putting them through the Point-of-Sale and always gets it right the first time. I operate at a faster rate, but my error rate is higher, which can result in customers getting the wrong drink or food order. I like Grace because she responds positively to my ideas. For example, I'm thinking about using the upstairs space as a Virtual Reality (VR) play zone and I've priced out some Oculus VR headsets with the intention of renting them out for thirty minutes at a time. This would give two additional revenue streams – one for the VR headset rental; the other for the drinks and food the customers would buy. As part of my market research, I ran the idea past the Saturday student staff as I thought putting such an idea to a Gen-Z cohort would have stirred a bit of enthusiasm. But the response from the first two I ask was underwhelming:

"We don't have enough time to hire out VR helmets," said one.

"It might be really disturbing for the other customers," said another.

Two negatives, but two more to ask. My expectations were high for a positive response from Brian – he's a twenty-year-old student and talks a lot about gaming.

"Would you or your friends come to a Virtual Reality cafe, Brian?" I ask.

"Not really. I've already got a VR helmet and a friend has a Vive XR headset. That's the best one on the market. So, we wouldn't really be interested."

Grace walked into the group at this time, and I asked her the same questions.

"I think that would be awesome," she said.

At last, a positive response. Although one out of four is not the hit rate I was hoping for. Maybe I should target the middle-aged market rather than the more switched-on youngsters.

Today is proving to be a typical Sunday, with steady footfall and occasional lulls. This makes it a good coffee training day and the students love this. Unlike many coffee shops, we don't allow staff to prepare drinks for customers until they have demonstrated their ability to create a smooth microfoam and pour it, so it produces a drink with consistent silkiness. I tell the girls they can practise and to try out some of the new latte varieties. Anyone would think I'd given them a Willy Wonka golden ticket. Imperfect speciality coffees and hot chocolates are produced – hazelnut hot chocolate with whipped cream and cappuccinos smothered (rather than dusted) with chocolate powder.

The Brummie Bikers arrive – two men who cycle from somewhere around Birmingham and stop off here every other week. I would estimate them to be in their late forties; both seem to be bulging out of their cycling lycra. We are in a pedestrianised zone, and they obviously cycle past at least two other local coffee shops to get here. They say they are stopping off for ten minutes and they order two flat whites and two tea cakes. Twenty minutes later, they order more coffee and a cake each, and relax in their window seat for another twenty minutes or so. They get up, bring their cups and plates back to the counter and thank us.

Lunch breaks occur between 11:00 and 2:00, one at a time, twenty minutes each. I tell Nia and Grace to decide between themselves who is to go first for their break, and so starts the politeness.

"You can go first if you like."

"I don't really mind. Do you want to go first?"

"What time is it now?"

Eventually, they settle it by playing rock-paper-scissors.

It's just past one o'clock and Bill comes in. Monday to Saturday he sits with two of his friends, but on Sunday he is normally on his own and enjoys chatting and banter with the staff. Someone told me he is eighty-five years old. I would have put him ten years younger. Grace takes his order for a brie and caramelised onion panini and a flat white.

"I'll make that for you, Bill," I say.

"Oh, you're going to make it?" he says.

"Yes, Louise has just gone for lunch."

"Oh dear! Well, I don't mind waiting."

"Trust me, Bill."

He takes a seat and starts reading his paperback. I dash into the kitchen and make his panini. I may be slower and messier than Louise, but what a customer loses in plate presentation they gain with a more generous filling. I assemble it on the plate and take it to Bill at his table.

Eventually, Bill stands up to leave, and comes back to the counter.

"Thank you, Steve, that panini was adequate."

"Always a pleasure, Bill."

One of the problems we sometimes encounter on a Sunday is running out of ingredients. This is because our food deliveries are twice a week – Monday and Thursday. We rely on these just-in-time deliveries due to our limited storage space. For example, the biggest storage item is part-baked ciabatta sandwich rolls (these being what are used for paninis and ciabatta sandwiches). They are frozen, and a box of thirty ciabattas is 40 x 30 x 27 centimetres. We will typically use six boxes between Thursday and Monday, which takes up a lot of freezer capacity. Our cakes and pastries are also frozen. We have two double, full-height freezers and after our Thursday delivery, they are both full.

Today, we have sufficient ciabattas, but we have run out of other ingredients, such as avocados, salad leaves and salad tomatoes. Jack, one of our regulars, is sitting outside waiting on his panini lunch and I must go out to apologise for not having salad and so offer him crisps on the side instead.

"Can't you just go to Waitrose and buy some more salad?" he says.

"Well, I could, but it means you'll be waiting a bit longer."

"That's fine." He pulls out his cigarette packet. "I'll just have a smoke. I'm in no hurry."

I run over to Waitrose and buy four cos lettuces and some cherry tomatoes, which I estimate will see us through until the delivery tomorrow. It's not uncommon for someone to have to do a Waitrose run, but this is probably the only time I've had to do it in the middle of preparing the order.

We stop serving at three o'clock and the cleaning routine starts. I show Priya how to operate the vacuum cleaner (I'm not sure if she's used one before) and I cash up the till. Takings are £790; £120 of that is VAT, which makes our net sales total for the day £670. Our Point-of-Sale System sends the sales data to our staff scheduling system (which also stores salary information). The staff cost ratio is 29%, which is excellent – the best cost ratio for the week. This is explained by the fact the students are on a lower rate of pay than the regular midweek permanent staff. Plus, I don't pay myself. If a manager were on duty instead of me, the staff cost ratio would have been closer to 39%, which is only borderline profitable.

The team leave at 3.30 p.m. I say goodbye and lock the door; I'll be here a while longer as I have some maintenance and routine end-of-week jobs to do. I start by replacing the water filter for the espresso machine, which I need to change approximately every three months (or after 10,000 litres has gone through). This takes thirty minutes as I need to flush through twenty litres of water to get rid of the cloudiness. Two fluorescent tube lights need changing upstairs as they are flickering; that involves unscrewing the housing unit and fitting the new ones. Then I move on to one of my routine Sunday afternoon jobs: compressing the waste. Our waste bin collections are Tuesdays and Thursdays – those are the only days that are available, which is less than ideal as most of the waste is generated between Thursday and Tuesday.

I climb into the large, 1,000-litre capacity bin and compress its contents by repeatedly tramping on it. This contains recyclable and general waste – cardboard packaging, empty plastic milk cartons; and food and coffee waste, which is bagged. I achieve a compression rate of something like 50%, which creates enough space for the waste packaging that will accumulate after our food delivery tomorrow. If I did not do this on a Sunday, then by Monday afternoon we would have overspill on the floor, which would be a breach of health and safety regulations.

I have one more maintenance job to do, which will have to wait for another day, and that is to defrost the freezers. The ice build-up on the freezer walls is about two inches thick, which further limits our frozen storage space. Sunday is the best day for defrosting as stock is at its lowest. I move everything in to one freezer, spray the empty one with de-icer and attempt to hack off blocks of ice using a knife, which invariably results in surface water and grubby footprints on the floor. It's a two-hour job and not one I have the time or motivation for this evening.

I remove the cash takings for the week from the safe under the till. I set the alarm, lock up and make my way to the car park. It will take me an hour to drive home.

When I get home, I count out the cash and put it in envelopes for banking on Monday. I reflect on a satisfactory day – good banter with the customers, great teamwork from the Sunday crew and my lemon drizzle cake proved popular, with one customer returning to buy a second slice and another customer coming in just before closing to buy two slices to take away. I start up my computer and send an email to Nia telling her I'm increasing her wages by £1 an hour in recognition of her experience in making coffee combined with her excellent customer service and her willingness to train the other girls on coffee. In truth, I don't want her to leave as it would take several weeks to train someone else up to that standard.

It's shortly after 8 p.m. when I settle down in front of the television with Sharon. I open a bottle of Rioja and pour a large glass, and a gin and tonic for Sharon.

"I don't know where you get your stamina from. I couldn't keep up with the Sunday shift," says Sharon.

"It was quite a good day in the shop today. Remember, Saturday and Sunday are our profitable days, so I need to keep them going," I say.

"We hardly have any time together and when we do, you can't relax as there always some problem at the coffee shop. You need to get one of the managers to do Sunday and start getting your weekends back."

"My plan is to make Louise the Sunday manager, but I'll keep it going for a little bit longer. Just until we get into profit."

"Don't you need to start going back to the office?"

"Not full-time, but yes, I need to start making an appearance."

The next thing I remember is Sharon prodding me awake from my sofa slumber. "I'm going to bed," she says.

I look at the clock. It's 10.30 p.m. For a moment, I thought it was Monday morning.

PART 3

CURVEBALLS

I have been running this place long enough to understand the impact of uncontrollable events. Some are good for business, such as craft markets, street parties and other community events. Then there are extreme weather events, such as gale-force winds or snowfall, which cause people to stay at home. Beyond that, the ebb and flow of customer traffic is mostly predictable. Warm weather, for instance, is good for business as it increases sales of homemade lemonade, iced lattes and frozen desserts. Customers can also cool off in the comfort of our air-conditioned premises, although we are now about to experience an 'extreme heat event.' This comes under the category of rare UK phenomenon and one I have not prepared for.

It's July 16th, and the UK government has issued a 'Level 4 heat health alert,' as temperatures are predicted to touch 40 degrees Celsius, and people (especially the elderly) have been advised to stay indoors. I sense this could have the same impact on business that a snow or storm day has.

The meteorological forecast is accurate, and people are heeding the stay-at-home advice. Our morning trade is slightly less than normal, but the lunchtime and afternoon trade have collapsed. Our midweek daily takings are normally in the range £900-£1,300.

I now have three consecutive days where takings have fallen below £600. Compounding the problem, we have had to throw away a large amount of fresh food that has gone past its use-by date or has become wasted due to the heat. We posted a half-price deal on Facebook for cakes, scones and pastries, but there were hardly any takers. Of course, we have the usual complement of staff on shift.

Just when I was starting to feel confident about our progress, a curveball strikes us. It's difficult to adapt to adverse climate days such as extreme heatwaves. I can't just tell the staff I don't need them for the next few days, nor do I imagine the landlord being very agreeable if I asked for a rent reduction on account of a temporary loss of footfall due to extreme weather. There are times when I feel I'm making progress with improving this business, then the unexpected happens, our cash flow takes a hit and I realise I still have a lot to learn, such as contingency planning for uncontrollable events. It's a bit like trying to patch up a hole in the roof of your home and just when you think you're making progress, a water pipe bursts and floods the house.

It's 1ˢᵗ August, 2022, and I am starting to question the wisdom of my weekend lifestyle.

Before I embarked on this coffee shop venture, my weekends would involve exercise, reading, meeting friends, country walks and comfort computer time. Now, I spend Saturday and Sunday working in the coffee shop, doing whatever is necessary to keep customer orders flowing – from clearing tables to preparing food. This has emerged as my strategy for reducing my staff wage bill – I work for free. It is having some beneficial effect as we are not losing as much money as we once were, but my working at weekends is not a viable long-term strategy. It's like active procrastinating whilst I ponder what radical course of action is needed to transform this business into a profit-making enterprise.

It's Tuesday 2nd August, and I'm in the shop. I come in less often during the week because I have used up almost all my holiday entitlement with my regular job, and my employer has started to have expectations of my presence in the office two days a week. My evenings are divided between coffee-shop administration and work commitments. Sometimes mental exhaustion causes me to collapse into bed in the hope that I will awaken in the morning with renewed energy and cognitive clarity.

We are fully staffed today, so I'm not needed behind the counter, and I sit at a corner table with my laptop open. I've downloaded all transactions for the last month into a spreadsheet ready for some data mining. I still enjoy the familiarity of the regular morning crowd, such as the school dads, the builders and Steve and Simon – I still don't know what the latter do for work, but they are in at 8.45 a.m. every morning. We always have a chat while they sip their americano and cappuccino.

The period between 9 and 10:45 a.m. is quiet, which makes it a good time to catch up with Kieran. We look at the performance metrics for the previous three months. The staff cost ratio, which was improving, is now back above 50%; average transaction costs remain the same, but cost of goods has increased, which is not surprising with all the wholesale price rises in recent months. I received an email from our milkman this morning notifying us of another price increase – the third in six months. The UK inflation rate has hit 10% now and hardly a day goes by without hearing the phrase, 'cost-of-living crisis.' I wouldn't be surprised if the staff asked for a pay rise, and I wouldn't blame them. I think they are aware that we're not making a profit (yet), so hopefully they'll hold back on that one. Consumers are becoming more sensitive to price rises so I hold back on raising our prices as I don't want us to become the most expensive coffee shop in town. Anyhow, it behoves us to become more efficient.

I ask Kieran how everything else is going with the shop.

"I heard you yelled at the staff on Saturday," he says.

"Well, that's probably an exaggeration. Three of them – Fiona, Brian and Carla – were chatting and not in the least bit interested in customers, so I split them up."

"They're still upset."

"They're probably in a huff because I put them on extra cleaning duty."

On reflection, perhaps I did raise my voice. It was a quiet period in the afternoon. I came out from the kitchen and saw three tables waiting to be cleared, a handful of customers at their seats and the loudest conversation was coming from behind the counter as the three of them were talking about university life, travel plans and boyfriends. I smacked the countertop to get their attention and told them to do the tables. They scattered, but within thirty seconds they had regrouped to continue their conversation.

"We might need to think about more customer service training for the weekend staff," I say. I'm not inclined to convey any apologies. "How about our Monday to Friday crew? Other than having to listen to Michelle's singing, are they happy?"

"Some of them are stressed because they need to train the two new people and get the orders out at the same time. There was another day last week when two staff had to go without their lunch break, which means they were working for ten hours. It's not fair on them."

"OK, I don't really want that sort of working environment. That's just pushing their loyalty too far." I'm tempted to say I never take a proper lunch break but hold my tongue on that one. "Are we still getting the orders out on time?"

"Sometimes the wait time goes to thirty minutes, so we stop taking food orders to clear the queue. On another day last week, we had to close the kitchen for the full day because one person phoned in sick. That took us down to four staff."

"Yes, I know about that. It's frustrating. You've seen the accounts. We're losing money, we need the food orders to survive. Couldn't we have put on a reduced menu?"

"There's still all the prep and cleaning to do. Running with five staff is stressful, four is impossible."

"You're right. I know that. That's just the way we do our food. But we also need to make some slightly more radical changes to shift patterns," I say.

"We've also had a lot of food go past its use-by date, so that just gets thrown out as waste."

"OK, I get it. That heatwave was a killer, but we have a big food prep problem to sort out and we need to think this through properly. In the meantime, let's get the new staff up to speed ASAP."

Kieran and I both understand the problem and there is no quick fix. Kieran's good at organising and hospitality but doesn't have the experience to make the big changes – the menu, the staffing and those precious procedures that slow us down. He's already punching above his weight, and I've dumped a lot of responsibility on him, including the management of sixteen staff. He is liked by most of the team, and it would be unfair to dump the dirty work on him, like renegotiating employment contracts. I could bring in the consultants we used during start-up – Andrew and Claire. They'll know what to do. They've run shops of this size before, and they are laser-focussed on profitability, but I will still need to be permanently present to drive through the changes and I don't want to lose our ethos of being a high-quality, community-focussed coffee shop. If I could take time out of my regular full-time job, it would be easier, but that would mean stopping my only source of income and that's a course of action I cannot afford. Another option is to take out a loan. Funding Circle recently sent me an invitation to apply for a business loan and I estimate that an injection of around £30,000 would allow me to recruit an experienced hospitality manager who could transform operations – everything from food preparation to shift patterns. I would give them a budget to work to and a bonus for hitting it. Kieran and I would learn from this person, and this would help us build a sustainable and profitable business, still much valued by our customer base. This wouldn't be throwing good money after bad because I know we have the footfall and a great reputation.

If there are two things I have learned since taking on this business nine months ago, they are: 1. how to make a decent latte and 2. how to generate a cash flow forecast. I've done both today; they each serve their intended purpose, but neither one looks pretty. My cash flow is irregular. I happily watch my bank balance grow as daily revenue deposits are made, then payroll comes out on the last Friday of the month. In July, the total staff costs, including pension payment and employer national insurance, amounted to £16,789. We have also just made a quarterly rent payment of £9,796 and a VAT payment of £12,820. When these three items coincide, the flourishing balance drops like a rock off a cliff edge. At the end of July, it sits at £4,903. There is no overdraft facility, but I do have a business credit card with a £10,000 limit, which I use to help with cash flow. The bottom line is, we are still solvent, but only just.

I walk behind the counter and make my second latte of the morning. I sit back down again, stare at my laptop screen and contemplate. It's 10.15 a.m. We have five staff here and the same number of customers. The staff are all busy doing things like folding napkins, wiping down the glass cake display and moving milk supplies from the main counter fridge to the one under the espresso machine, but no customer revenue is coming in. I take slight comfort from the fact that, within an hour, the morning hubbub will fire up and the energy levels will rise once again.

I reflect on the last nine months. We have had good ideas, and if we had followed through with plans and actions, we probably wouldn't be in the precarious position we now find ourselves in. Our successes include the upstairs refurbishment at the start of the year and building an artists' community. Where we have failed is on products and operations – our ideas, such as more homemade produce, bubble tea, grab-and-go lunch deals and mobile ordering and delivery haven't moved out of the station. Our strategy has been one of pushing the staff to become more efficient and working in the shop every weekend, which is creating more stress all round without achieving sustainable profit. Continuing on this path will lead to bankruptcy. This leaves me with three options:

- Take time off from my day job and work full-time in the business (optionally bringing consultants to help).
- Take out a business loan and recruit an experienced hospitality manager.
- Sell the business.

This is a big decision, and I would like to get a view from people who are in a good position to advise. First, my accountants.

I have two accountants. My official one is Michael. He prepares my official financial statements such as the balance sheet and profit & loss and submits my annual return to Companies

House. He is a seasoned accountant and I ask him about business valuations, and we have a technical conversation on asset depreciation methods. He has mentioned to me that he has other clients who run coffee shops and "they are making good money." I like Michael's formality and discipline. I can't imagine him not wearing a shirt and tie and he is the sort of person who, if you were to see him in the street or in a coffee shop, you would guess he is an accountant.

Then there is Zoe – my other accountant, who helps me day-to-day with all things financial. She has been good counsel since our early start-up phase: reviewing our business plan, keeping me honest with bookkeeping and sorting out the monthly payroll. Zoe does not take any form of payment (unless you include the fine wine we consume on a heavy evening at our house).

I'm fortunate to have Zoe. She is a Group Finance Director for a global company and has many commitments and a high level of responsibility. I feel like I'm asking the chief navigator of an ocean-going liner to help out on a children's boating lake. I'm grateful. More importantly, Zoe is streetwise and knows how businesses should be managed and gets to the heart of why they underperform. She also carries a reputation. "Ballbreaker" was the term I once heard. She can dissect my accounts with ease, has little tolerance for incompetence and talks without any form of profanity filter. Thankfully, she has a good understanding of how our business is performing and is well-placed to advise.

Zoe and her husband Mark have come round one Friday night, and the conversation quickly turns to the turmoil of the coffee shop. In the early days of our venture, she reassured me that most businesses start off making a loss and it always takes time to turn a profit. There are no such words of reassurance tonight.

"Steve, you can't run a business with these staff costs, you need to get in there and change things around," she says.

"Yep, I know. I'm thinking that through, but it's not just staff. There are other things we can do – reduce wastage for a start."

"How much is getting wasted?"

"Sometimes it's carelessness. Last week, we had to throw away a pack of Wiltshire ham because it wasn't stored in a sealed container. So, we need to put in place a better food rotation system."

"What the *<swear word>*! Why are you pissing around with crap like that when you're losing nearly two thousand pounds a month? Food waste isn't your *<swear word>* problem."

I feel she has me pinned to the wall and will hold me there until I promise to make the tough decisions needed to turn around this business.

We have finished three bottles of wine between us, and the way we are all feeling, we'll get through three more before the night is out. Zoe continues to be unambiguously direct with her advice, none of which I can refute.

It's Tuesday 16th August. The staff have gone home now, I've locked up and I'm in the shop alone. It's still 30 degrees outside, so I'm thankful to be enjoying the comfort of an air-conditioned environment. My visitor arrives, John from Midland Business Services, who specialises in the valuation and sale of businesses and commercial properties.

"Just to be straight with you, John, I've not decided to put the business up for sale yet. It's just an option and I would like a view on its valuation," I say.

"You've got a nice place here and it's in a great location. Is the equipment yours or on lease?"

"Everything is owned by me."

He nods his head in approval and takes notes.

"So, why are you thinking of selling it? Personal reasons?"

"It's loss-making." I decide to be fully transparent as I would rather get a worst-case valuation. "It never used to be. It's been running at a profit for ten years under the previous ownership, but so many costs have gone up and I'm struggling to dedicate the time it really needs."

"Okay, well could you show me around first, then we'll look at the accounts."

I give him a tour, pointing out all the high-cost equipment, such as the two full-height double freezers, two speed ovens, passthrough dishwasher, two high-spec espresso machines. I need to make sure John appreciates the value of the equipment, fixtures and fittings,

"I've done a rough estimate of replacement value for all this kit, and it's in the region of eighty thousand. If you were to do a complete fit-out from scratch, including furnishings, you'd be looking at something in the region of one hundred and fifty thousand," I say.

He looks around the shop. "There's nothing much wrong with what you have." He points towards the sofa diagonally opposite. "These sofas look almost new," he says.

"They are, although some of our other furniture is a bit charmless, but it's comfortable enough." We sit back down, and he places his notepad on the table.

"There are two ways to value a business. One is by asset value – that's all your equipment, fixtures and fittings – the other is a multiple of annual profits. For example, four times your annual net profit," he says.

"Well, option two's not going to work because I'm loss-making.

I'm not ready to just give it away."

"Hold on." He raises his hand, palm facing towards me. "If you were to go ahead with the sale, we would value it based on *potential* profitability. So, we look at your revenue and your fixed costs such as rent. Then we would derive a benchmark cost for staff, cost of goods, etc., based on industry average, and that will give us potential profitability. We'll take a multiple based on that."

"What sort of people would you market it to?"

"This looks like a business that would be well-suited to a couple who would work here full-time."

"I agree."

We start talking about accounts and cash flow and I show him our last VAT return, which gives us a reliable view of our revenue, then I show him the latest Profit & Loss statement from our accounting system. The fact we are loss-making doesn't seem to be an issue so long as we have a decent revenue stream. He calculates what he believes would be a realistic valuation – £65,000. That is £5,000 more than I paid for the business (although I have spent over £10,000 on improvements).

I thank him for his time and helpful explanations of the current market for coffee shops. He isn't pushy and he says I should just give him a call if I need to talk some more about the sale of the business. We shake hands and say goodnight.

It is Saturday 20th August. Unusually, I've taken a day off from the shop, which is unfortunate because on this day one staff member called in to say they have a virus, and another has had to go home mid-morning due to being sick (in the staff toilet, thankfully). With two people short, the kitchen is closed. I discover this in the afternoon after receiving an email from a regular customer who is complaining about our inability to serve food.

Saturday is the worst day to close the kitchen and I estimate the revenue loss for the day to be in the region of £500. I realise that I now need to make the choice between my regular full-time job (which pays a regular salary, including paid holiday) and the coffee shop. Both are full-time commitments. The trouble is, I'm not sure I have the energy, motivation or the perseverance to keep running this business, which leaves me with a Hobson's choice.

It's Monday morning, and I phone John to tell him my decision. I am quick to agree with the sales particulars, and the business is on the market under a confidential sale. This is a sad decision for me; but all things considered, it is the right one. As John said, this is a business that would suit a couple or two people in partnership, who would be here to manage it full-time. I have run my race and failed to finish. It now needs someone new, who has the experience and passion to bring out its true value.

The next thing I do is sit down with Kieran and tell him the news. This is sensitive because, for a second time, it looks like I'm putting him out of work. I explain that the new owner, whoever that may be, will have to take on the existing staff so his job is safe. To my surprise, he takes the news without any fear or adverse reaction.

"I can see the business is losing money. Maybe I'll be able to learn more about business and hospitality management from the new owner," he says.

"That would be a positive, and you know what, you've built up some great experience here over the last year, so if you wanted to look elsewhere, you have some great experience for hospitality or retail management," I say.

I think I sense a feeling of relief. Although he's made friends and enjoys the responsibility of management, he is often the buffer between the staff and me and has to absorb their gripes and grievances.

"Courtney might be upset, though. She's really settled here," he says.

"Ah, right." I'd not thought of that. "Well, perhaps you can explain what's happening to the business. Hopefully, she'll understand." This could be awkward.

IMPENDING CLIFF EDGE

Friday 26th August, 2022: I am fifty-eight years old today. Normally, Sharon and I would celebrate by going out for a nice meal or meeting up with friends and generally enjoying the bank holiday weekend. However, right now, three things are causing me angst: 1. Increasing demands from my regular job; 2. The business bank balance continues to shrink, and 3. Wondering how I'm going to find a buyer for this loss-making business.

My employer operates a large Life Sciences organisation, and my job is to manage a cyber security team who, amongst other things, test systems to uncover security weaknesses. Over the last nine months, I have been successfully working remotely, whilst keeping on top of deadlines and turning up at important meetings. Last week, Ray, who is in my team, called to give me a 'heads-up' on a meeting with some internal customers. Someone said that I wasn't really focused on my projects anymore and I couldn't explain a missed delivery date. The tide has turned on the work-from-home culture. Three months ago, when I went into the office, I was the only person sitting amongst a bank of twenty hot desks. Now, most people are in at least three days a week. This puts me at a disadvantage as I'm less connected to the day-to-day goings on. My team always keep me abreast of issues and I can normally jump on a video call at a moment's notice, but low office visibility is now considered an indicator of non-commitment. I take this as an early warning sign and, a bit like an unresponsive website, it's something I need to fix.

Today's payroll run, including taxation and pensions, amounted to £15,870 and our bank balance is £10,946. I will work out the staff cost ratio at month end, but I estimate it will be around 50%, which means another loss-making month. Our operational performance was getting better, but a combination of uncontrollable events and sudden staff absences has set us back. My cash flow forecast tells me the business will remain solvent until January (assuming I keep working at weekends and we have no more uncontrollable adverse events). That is when three big bills become due, specifically quarterly rent of £9,796, VAT in the region of £12,000 and the monthly payroll of approximately £16,000. There will be enough money for two of those items, but not all three. Bankruptcy will not affect me personally, as this is a limited liability company: but the doors will close, all staff will be out of a job until a buyer comes along and picks up the business and its assets at a fire sale – and I can't think of anything more demoralising. As for the sale of the business as an ongoing concern, I cling to the hope that there is someone out there with the finance, experience and passion to take on this business as it is.

The confidentiality status of my proposed sale lasted for three days. Two customers discreetly asked Kieran about it as they had heard it was on their market through their business networks. I assume the secret is out, so I send an email to all staff to inform them of my decision. I kept it short and sweet:

Dear Team,
I have decided to put the coffee shop up for sale. This is
a sad decision for me, but I find I am unable to dedicate
the time needed to run this business. I am hopeful of
finding a new owner with the experience and the time
to bring the best out of Arden's. Rest assured, your jobs
will be safe as whoever buys the business will have to
honour your existing terms and conditions of employ-
ment. If you have any questions or concerns, I'll be
happy to chat with you.

I arrive at the shop just after 8.30 a.m. on the Saturday morning. I'm anticipating an unsettled atmosphere so I skipped the park run this morning as I feel I should be in the shop in case anyone wants to talk. As I walk in, everything seems normal, with two staff on the floor and three behind the counter. Two more student staff are due to start at 11 a.m. and that should help the expected lunchtime surge.

I wave to Lucy and Fiona, who are behind the counter. "Morning," I say.

"Hi Steve," they both say in unison, showing no sign of anxiety.

This may be easier than I thought. I walk into the kitchen area. Courtney's on food-prep. "Morning, Courtney," I say. She glances round briefly and turns away without uttering a word. Kieran did mention that she was taking the news of the sale badly. I sense the emotional impact this is having and remind myself I have some fences to mend while still searching for a buyer.

During the mid-morning quiet period, I ask Courtney to join me upstairs. I start by explaining that the business is losing money, I'm worn out, and I need to start focussing on my regular job again. It wasn't a cry for sympathy, just a chance for a chat and for me to listen to her.

"I enjoy working here and I've made some good friends. I was just upset when I heard you're going to sell the place," she says.

"Well, whatever happens, you'll still have your job. Any new owner will have to keep you and Kieran on, unless you decide to leave and go elsewhere. Remember, you've built up some good experience here and there's nothing to stop you getting another job," I say.

"I understand. It must be difficult because you've got your other job," she says.

We're back on speaking terms after our chat and we head downstairs together. The Saturday staff are continuing as though nothing is changing. I talk to Lucy and Carla, who both seemed relaxed.

"I wasn't surprised when I found out," says Lucy. "I noticed you stayed behind after hours the other day and thought it would be something like that."

I leave shortly after the lunchtime rush, which is earlier than usual for a Saturday, but I am back in tomorrow for my long Sunday shift. John informs me that there have been some enquiries, but I haven't had any viewing requests yet, although it's not even been on the market for a week. I'm hopeful that by the end of the year, Arden's will become someone else's problem.

The following Saturday, when I'm back in the shop, a husband and wife, whom I recognise as occasional customers ask if they could have a chat with me. Their daughter, Chloe, used to work here, and she left in a bit of a sulk. They introduce themselves as Andrew and Tracy and they claim to be enquiring on behalf of 'friends' who are interested in purchasing the coffee shop, with the intention of running it as a family business.

"Are they local? I'm here all day if they want to do a viewing," I say.

"Oh, that's okay," says Tracy, "we spoke to them this morning and they asked if we could bring back the details. They know we come here a lot and I said we know you, and we'd speak to you and bring back all the info."

They're not putting on a very convincing charade. It's quite clear that they have designs on taking over this place themselves, together with their high-maintenance daughter.

"The first thing to tell your friends is that managing a place like this is tough. It really is a full-time job and that's why I'm selling up. I don't have the time to run it anymore," I say.

"Chloe says it's a bit disorganised downstairs," says Tracy.

"It just needs a good manager," says Andrew.

Good manners prevent me from being fully transparent about their daughter's suitability for management. She resigned shortly after I took over, and in that time, she demonstrated an aptitude for work avoidance, a talent for gossip and an indifference to common courtesy. I recall one day, when she was on the till, a customer came back to the counter with his pot of tea.

"I'm sorry, but this tea isn't very hot," he said.

"It was hot when we made it," she said.

"Well, I've just poured it and it's lukewarm."

"I'm just saying, it was hot when we served it," she replied.

The customer was eventually given a fresh pot of tea and an apology. Chloe was given some guidance on customer service, which by all accounts passed from one eardrum to the other without stimulating any brain cells. Memories of Chloe's tomfoolery come flooding back, like a haunting we failed to exorcise. I do recall her making friends with a couple of the weekend staff, but she seemed oblivious to her unpopularity with everyone else. If she were to return as a manager, I suspect most of the staff would either resign or stay on for comedy value.

I remind myself that this is business and I'm not able to pick and choose my buyers, but I wish these two would just be honest with me. It feels as though they are treating me like a fool.

"I tell you what, let me take you through the profit and loss and some of the business metrics." We spend the next twenty minutes going through all the costs and the revenue stream. "As you can see, we are losing approximately two thousand pounds a month," I say.

Andrew leans back in his chair and smiles. "Our friends have run a business before and will be able to sort this place out," he says.

They show no signs of discouragement. If anything, their enthusiasm has grown stronger. I hand over a copy of the accounts and full details of the sale. Tracy takes them from me, almost in the same way a child takes a present from Santa Claus.

"Thank you. We'll be in touch," says Tracy.

"Let us know if anyone else decides to make an offer," says Andrew.

They leave without leaving contact details. Who knows? Maybe their friends aren't imaginary and will contact me for a viewing.

It's Tuesday evening. The staff have gone home, and I am alone in the shop working on my laptop. I'm expecting visitors, a young couple who are driving up from London, as they are interested in buying the shop. Asali and Hazeem were due at 7 p.m., but message me to say they will be about an hour late due to heavy traffic. They finally arrive along with four other family members. Hazeem tells me he works in a busy coffee shop in the city. He is impressed by the fact we have two espresso machines, multiple grinders and serve loose-leaf tea. I sense he is an experienced barista. His wife, Asali, says she works in business, whatever that means. They are recently married and are looking to run their own coffee shop and are happy about the prospect of relocating to Kenilworth. I give them the full tour. The two of them ask about all the equipment. One of the older family members asks if he can see my latest VAT return and copies of the latest electricity bill. Another family member takes pictures of the digital menu displays. They spend over an hour in the shop. Hazeem and Asali are unable to hide their excitement.

"Okay, this is exactly what we are looking for," says Haseem.

"It would be a great business for a couple," I say.

"Have you had any other interest?" says Asali.

"Yes, I have another viewing on Saturday evening and one other party has shown interest," I say.

"Well, we can move quickly. What is the buy-it-now price?" says Asali.

"It's sixty-five thousand, but I'm doing everything through the agency and my solicitor. Have you seen the accounts?"

"Yes, we've got them from the agent," says Asali. She looks at the older family member, who nods his head in confirmation.

"So, would you be able to stay on and train us up on everything?" asks Haseem.

"Of course, but you would be best to learn from my son, Kieran. Are you aware that the staff will be transferred to you through the TUPE rules?"

"Oh yes, we definitely need the staff," says Haseem.

It's almost 10 p.m. when I lock up and drive home. I'm exhausted but happy at the thought I may have just sold the business, without trying too hard. They seem like a nice couple.

Next morning, just after 11 a.m., I receive a call from John at Midland Business Services.

"Good news, Steve. I've just had Asali on the phone, and they have offered the full asking price. You obviously did a good job of selling it to them."

"When I didn't hear from you first thing this morning, I was worried that they may have changed their minds. It's nice to get some good news for a change."

"Well, they want to move quickly. Now, regarding their finances, they are getting a loan from a family member, so once I've seen evidence of funds, we can go into contract negotiations."

"Okay. Anything you can do to push things along will be appreciated, John."

"I'll keep you updated," he says.

John estimates it will take approximately two months to go through the legal process and exchange contracts, but "that depends on how quickly the solicitors respond to enquiries," he says. I don't need reminding of that indeterminate legal process. We are in the first week of September and if we complete the sale before Christmas, we will remain financially solvent. That must be doable. I'm feeling relieved as it allows me to focus more on my Monday to Friday day job, whilst still coming in at weekends.

Two days later, I receive an email from Andrew and Tracy. They tell me their friend has looked through the accounts and concluded it requires too much of an investment. However, if I were to reduce the asking price, they may be interested. I reply to the effect that I have just accepted an offer for the full asking price, and I sign it with two smiley face emojis.

It's Tuesday 20th September and I'm in London. I walk through a car park towards the large double glass sliding doors, which open automatically, allowing me access to the atrium of our head office. A few people are seated on sofas, browsing their smartphones. Another six or so are standing in line at the glossy white reception desk, each waiting to get photographed before their visitor pass is issued. I stride past them, stop at the entrance barriers and stare into the facial recognition camera. A dashboard light flashes green and the message, 'successfully authenticated' is displayed. The barrier opens, I enter, and a uniformed guard wishes me good morning. He recognises me because he has worked here for the last twenty years, as have I.

I am now in what is known as 'the avenue' – a large open-plan area that forms a channel through the centre of the building. There are windowed offices on each side, which stretch four storeys high to meet a glass roof. There is a coffee shop at each end and numerous meeting booths, cube sofas and chairs of varying colours provide meeting spaces. To my right is a large alcove, signposted, 'help hub.' A wheeled, white robot coasts back and forth, like a sentry at a palace. It has a large digital display with the words, 'Ask me Anything.'

I navigate round the indoor trees and stone water features towards the horseshoe- shaped coffee bar. Thankfully, they still have a traditional espresso machine and human baristas. Magdalena is on coffee duty today.

I walk up to the counter. "Good morning, Magda," I say.

"Hello, Steve," she says. "It's so nice to see you. I thought you'd left the company and hadn't said goodbye."

"I would never do that, Magda. I've just had other commitments recently, but that's a story for another time. You'll probably see more of me from now on."

"That will be nice." She reaches for a carton of oat milk. "Oat milk latte?"

"Please. And put an extra shot in that. I might need it today."

"Busy day ahead?"

"A couple of meetings then a security review of a new machine learning algorithm."

She swirls the milk into the cup and finishes it off with tulip-style latte art. "This should keep you going." She places the cup on a saucer and places it on the counter.

"That looks perfect." I pick up my drink and sit at an empty table.

The head office is almost back to the pre-pandemic hustle and bustle. When I was last here, the foot traffic on the avenue was mostly that of facilities staff who clean the windows and water the plants. Now, it's buzzing with corporate conversations and people heading in different directions. It's not quite the hubbub of laughter and chatter I've become accustomed to in Arden's, more of a murmuring of management speak and the three-letter acronyms which make up the vernacular in this place: lead indicators, KPIs, launch dates and milestones. I sip my latte and begin to immerse myself in this familiar environment. I have friends and colleagues here, some of whom I've known for years. I've lived through many changes and immediately feel back at home, navigating the challenges and conflicts of this corporate life. I feel I'm back in my comfort zone. Casual business attire is the order of the day. Looking around, I suspect there is a menswear fashion retailer who is doing a good trade in light blue shirts and navy-blue trousers. There is a bit more colour variety amongst the ladies – dresses, blouse and skirt or trouser suit. Sitting at an adjacent table to me are two men. One, I would estimate to be in his mid-forties; the other, I would say is in his mid-twenties, tall, bearded with long hair tied back in a ponytail; he is sketching what looks like a flowchart on his notepad, presumably explaining a process or system to his older colleague.

I see Rachel – my meeting partner – walking towards me. She sits down and stares at me through her retro-style, thick-rimmed glasses.

"Hello, stranger," she says.

She places her two iPhones on the table, and points to my coffee cup. "Would you like another?"

"Thanks, but I've reached my caffeine capacity for the day."

My phone vibrates in my pocket; I ignore it.

Rachel is one of my stakeholders – a bit like a customer, friendly but demanding. My team performs cyber security assessments for software created by her team. We are meeting to discuss how my team can speed up our security assessments and take on even more work without increasing headcount.

"The research scientists have put in two new requests for data workflows, and we need to deliver before year end. We can deliver, but we need your team to turn round your security assessments quicker," she says.

One of Rachel's phones pings and she glances at the display.

"I haven't got enough headcount, Rachel. If you have some budget, I could pull someone in quite quickly," I say.

She shakes her head. "The budget's been fully committed for this year. We need to find a way to streamline or just work smarter," she says.

I amuse myself at the thought of how the tables have turned on me. In Arden's, I'm the one asking staff to work quicker and smarter. Now I'm on the receiving end. This is karma, I guess.

We chat through some ideas, but wrap up our meeting without any agreement and she's not happy. "Let me look at our project scheduler. Maybe we catch up later?" I say.

She looks at her phone. "I've got back-to-back meetings for the rest of the day," she says.

"Okay, well let me see what I can work out. I'll chat to the team and drop you an email later," I say.

She walks off. I pick up my laptop and walk towards the staircase. I wave to Magda at the coffee counter. "Bye, Magda."

"Bye, Steve, take care," she replies.

The day they replace the baristas with robots will be the day I retire. I grab a banana and an apple from the free fruit basket, climb to the first floor, claim a vacant hot desk, sit down and make a start on my morning emails. My phone vibrates again; I pull it out of my pocket. It's a message from Hazeem, asking me to phone him. I have a momentary panic that they've encountered a problem and he is calling to say they can no longer buy the coffee shop. I escape into a meeting pod and call him.

"Steve, thanks for calling back. I just want to confirm a few things with you if that's all right?"

"Sure. How can I help?"

"Could we arrange a two-week training period before we officially take over?" he says.

"I suppose so. As I said before, Kieran and the other supervisors would be best to do that."

"The thing is, once we take over, we'll have to put all the staff on notice and it's likely we'll do that on day one, that way we can run it ourselves from day one," he says.

"I thought you said you'll be keeping most of the staff," I say.

"It's financial. You said yourself the staff costs were too high," he says.

Now I'm getting worried. "I would caution you against doing that so soon, Haseem, as there's quite a lot to learn and you'll need to keep the permanent staff at least."

"So, let me tell you what we're thinking. We could manage the place for you during those two weeks before the official handover, and you can train us."

"You mean before we exchange contracts?"

"Exactly. It will be the quickest way for us to do handover and transition. Then we can deal with the staffing problem."

"Well, we'd have to put something in place legally." I'm suddenly panicking. I don't want to lose this sale, but this sounds a bit underhand. "Let me come back to you on that one," I say.

Everything seemed cut and dried when we agreed the sale two weeks ago. Now he wants to put all the staff on notice on day one, and I've already told the staff their jobs will be safe! He also wants to run the place for me before legal completion. What if he changes his mind and walks away? This morning started so well. I call John from the agency and relay my conversation with Hazeem.

"I don't want to lose this sale, John, but I'm not happy about his approach to sacking the staff. And he wants to get hands-on in the shop before we complete the sale."

As usual, his advice is direct. "Don't start any training or handover activities until contracts have been exchanged and monies transferred," he says.

"Do you think they're having second thoughts or trying to pull a fast one?"

"Let me talk to them and I'll get to the bottom of it," he says.

Just when I was feeling confident and motivated about being back in the office, another curveball comes my way. This one short phone call has caused my mental focus to switch back to coffee shop dilemmas once again.

Next morning, a little after 10 a.m., my phone vibrates. I see it's John and I answer it instantly.

"Hi, John."

"Steve, I'm afraid I've got some bad news," he says.

"Go on."

"They really want the place but the family member who promised them the finance has pulled out and they are now twenty grand short of the asking price."

This does not come as a shock; in fact, I've been awake most of the night in anticipation of this conversation. "That explains why they wanted to run the place for me before exchange," I say.

"It was Asali I was talking to. She's the one dealing with all the finances. I did tell her she should have had her finances fully agreed before jumping in with an offer."

"So, I'm back to square one," I say.

"Not quite, there are a couple of interested parties who contacted me recently asking if the business is still available, so let me follow up with them," he says.

Part of me is feeling relieved as I don't think I could have faced going back to the staff to tell them the new owners wanted to get rid of them as quickly as possible. The customers wouldn't take kindly to such an action either. This is a Kenilworth coffee shop, where customers value familiarity and staff who know their name and usual order.

This moment is probably my biggest setback. One minute I had a good-faith buyer for the business, now I'm back looking at an impending cliff edge. After running the September payroll, the bank balance is down to £7,150. The rent is covered until December, but according to my cash flow forecast, January will be the point when we become insolvent. If a credible buyer doesn't materialise soon, I might as well just give this business away for free.

END GAME

It's Saturday 1st October. Ten days have passed since the fall-out from the sale that never was. I've done two viewings in that time, but neither party wish to progress. I have another viewing shortly after closing time today. I'm feeling despondent and my expectations for this next viewing aren't high.

Iris and Tom arrive at 5.30 p.m. I would estimate them to be in their mid-forties, both of slim build, wearing jeans and casual tops and jackets. I think they have been here before as customers, but I can't be certain. They say they live in Warwick, about five miles away.

"Shall we start with a tour of the premises?" I say.

"Yes please," they both reply at once.

I helped with the end of day cleaning today and everything looks good. In fact, I don't think the customer toilets have ever been so clean. We climb the stairs and I talk about the arrangement we have with the Kenilworth artists.

"I like this. Will they be willing to keep the exhibition after you leave?" asks Iris.

"I'm sure they'd be delighted," I say.

Iris is asking most of the questions: "Who supplies all the food?" She takes notes in a small, hardback notebook. "Are you leaving the salad bar and all the kitchen equipment?"

"It's being sold as a walk-in, ready-to-go business," I say.

"What does that do?" She points to the frozen dessert maker.

"That's for ice cream, sorbet and frozen yogurt. You insert a frozen dessert pod, press the button and a tub of ice cream or sorbet or frozen yogurt is produced. Would you like to try one?"

"Oh, yes. Mango sorbet please," she says.

I grab a pod from the freezer, insert it into the machine, put a tub under the dispenser, press the button and the sorbet comes out as a whirl. I hand it to her with a small plastic spoon.

She tastes a small amount and nods her head in approval.

"Why are you selling up, Steve?" Tom asks. He stands with his arms folded, as if challenging me to give a credible answer.

"I have a full-time job and I work in London a lot. I've realised that I can't run this place and do my that job at the same time. There's great potential here for someone who has the time and passion," I say.

"How was business today?"

"Over £1,600. I can show you the revenue day by day." I point to my laptop, sitting on the table with the screen open.

The three of us sit down at the table and I log into our Point-of-Sale website. The first screen shows the takings for the day – £1,653 – along with a graph showing the volume of sales for each hour of the day. An arrow flips to the previous day, and the one before that. Tom looks closely at the screen. Iris continues to eat her sorbet. Her notebook is closed, and she places it on the table.

"How many staff do you have on each day?"

"We open with three, then five or six for the middle of the day and typically close with four. There's a lot of room for efficiency," I say.

"And why did your original buyer pull out?" asks Tom.

"They lost their source of funding and couldn't make the purchase. They were seeking finance from elsewhere, but they weren't really in a good financial position, so we dropped them and put it back on the market."

"You are looking for someone with deep pockets then?" Tom asks.

"I'm looking for a reliable buyer with secured funding."

"Are you open to negotiating on price?"

"It's already priced to sell. The asking price is lower than the value of the equipment, so not at this stage."

"We are cash buyers and can move quickly. So, what will you accept?"

I pause to make a show of serious thought and calculation. I think I can read this negotiation. Iris has decided she wants this place, that is clear. In fact, she probably made her mind up before even stepping through the door. Tom likes the thrill of negotiation. If this were a poker game, I would win through reading their body language. I can detect their excitement, and even though I have the worst possible hand, they can't see my vulnerability. If I dig my heels in, I'm sure they'll fold. Where else can they purchase a fully functioning coffee shop at this price? But then again, how many cash buyers are willing to buy a loss-making business?

"Okay, as you are a cash buyer, I'll take five grand off the price," I say.

Tom smiles, slowly holds out his hand and we shake on the deal. He looks at his wife. She is smiling. They don't know it, but I'm probably the happiest of us all.

$$\backsim\!\!\!\!-\!\!\!\!\rightarrow$$

It's 6th November. It is one year since I took ownership of Ardens and three weeks since I agreed the sale with Tom and Iris. They are as keen to take over as I am to exit. Until then, I am happy to pull shots and prepare paninis.

Our respective solicitors are communicating with predictable pedantry and indeterminate delays between correspondence. My solicitor, who was very responsive one year ago, is the main offender this time, as despite giving assurances that he would have the contract drafted and sent out two weeks ago, nothing has materialised. He didn't respond to my emails for a week and was unable (or unwilling) to take my calls when I phoned his office. I sent him an email yesterday saying if he doesn't respond and give me a firm date for the contract, I will be forced to change solicitor. He responded in the middle of the night to say there is a lot of documentation to prepare but all contract documents will be prepared and sent to the buyer's solicitor by the end of next week. I am thankful that I don't need to change solicitor as that would just add more delay. My sense of urgency is not simply driven by the perilous state of the business finances or my inability to juggle two jobs, it's also the fear that my buyers will suddenly change their minds and drop out. I feel I'm crossing a river gorge on a tightrope, edging closer to the other side, but a sudden change in wind direction will send me careering into the rapids below.

It's Sunday, which means another day working in the coffee shop. Thankfully, my regular Sunday crew are still in place – Louise, Nia, Grace and Priya. They don't need any training and little supervision. Nia always jumps on the barista station; Grace does the till and sorts out cakes and Priya does everything from blending smoothies to serving tables. They all tag-team quite well. Some of Nia's family members are in this morning and have ordered food and drinks. They seem to be enjoying the novelty of Nia serving them. Just as she walks away after serving them at the table, one raises his hand. "Could you get me some sugar please, Nia?" Then, "Another pot of Earl Grey please, Nia."

Bill has come in and is sitting in one of the centre tables. As is often the case on a Sunday, he is on his own, but seems content reading a paperback. His soup and sandwich should be out in a few minutes. He catches my eye and raises his finger towards me. I go over to say hello. He probably wants to taunt me about something.

"Nice to see you, Bill. How are you?" I say.

"Well, I'm OK, but tell me, what's happening with the sale, Steve?" He closes his paperback and places it on the table.

"We've found new buyers. A nice couple. We're still going through the legal process; it may be another four weeks or so."

"Oh," he touches the side of my arm. "I was hoping you were going to tell me you had changed your mind and had decided to keep it." His arm shakes slightly, and his facial expression drops from hope to sadness.

I pause before responding. "I'm going to miss this place, Bill, but I've been working crazy hours and I'm losing money. It's just become too much for me."

"Well, I can understand that." He nods his head in empathy to my situation. "Your girls are lovely here, but I can see it's a difficult business. I just want to say I'll be sad to see you go."

"I'm sad too. I hope the new owners will keep the community spirit going."

"Well, it's not going to be quite the same."

"Thank you, Bill. That means a lot to me."

I may be stressed, skint and ready to drop, but I also feel emotional about leaving. I've developed a fondness for regulars like

Bill, for whom Arden's is like a home extension and the staff are dear friends.

Today has been a good Sunday trading day. We opened at 9.30 a.m. and closed at 3 p.m. The takings are £750 and, importantly, the staff cost ratio for the day is a respectable 32%. If only every day could be so profitable, I wouldn't be in this situation. The girls leave at 3.30 p.m. I don't have any maintenance today, so once I compress the rubbish in the waste bins, I lock up the shop then pop into Waitrose to buy a nice bottle of red wine before driving home.

It's Monday 29th November, and we are on the verge of exchanging contracts on the sale. I have sent over all the prerequisites, the most important item being the staff listing, which gives details such as contracted hours, hourly rate of pay and outstanding holiday allowance. Under TUPE rules, they will have to honour the terms and conditions of employment. However, an issue has arisen. Kieran is a working director of the company, and their solicitor has raised this as an issue and recommended that Kieran does not get transferred as an employee. Everything seemed to be going so well and now we have this eleventh-hour issue.

"I would recommend you keep Kieran on, at least for a month or so because he's the one who knows how everything works. He's the best person to train you up," I say.

"Our solicitor has stated that it would not be appropriate to transfer a director and we agree, so we have to hold firm on this," Tom says.

Once again, I find myself in the position of putting my own son out of work. He's relocated to Kenilworth and put a lot into this job, stepped in when I needed him and won round the staff who were so resistant to our takeover at the start.

"Okay, Tom, I understand. I was going to use him to train you up and help with the handover, but I'll pay him for the next month and that will give him a chance to find another job," I say.

The next phone call I make is to Kieran, to tell him to dust off his CV.

It's Sunday 4th December, 2022 – one year and one month after my first day at Arden's. My cash flow forecast is proving accurate. There is currently £5,459 in the bank. Thankfully, the fear of impending insolvency has passed as this is my last day of ownership. I send out an all-staff email on Friday, again keeping it short and sweet:

> *As you are aware, I recently found buyers for the business. I can now confirm that the sale has gone through and from Monday, Tom and Iris will become the new owners. I'm going to miss the buzz of the shop, the camaraderie of the team and the warmth of the customers.*
>
> *My last day in the shop will be Sunday. However, you may not have seen the last of me. For my next project, I intend to write a book – a memoir about my experiences running a coffee shop.*

I am here with my Sunday crew – Louise, Nia, Grace and Priya. Louise hits out the paninis and ciabattas, Nia produces artistic-looking lattes and the rest of us play tag-team between counter duties and table service. I have switched the background playlist to Christmas music, which has created a feel-good, festive vibe. Decorations, which I bought last year, are still boxed up; the new owners can choose what to do with them. We have a steady stream of regular, occasional and passer-by customers, including the Brummie bikers, dry cappuccino man, the personal trainers and side-salad Jack. Most of them have no knowledge that tomorrow, Arden's will be under new ownership.

Tom and Iris come in shortly before closing time. I take them upstairs as we have a lot of handover tasks to do. I have printed out a list of all the computer system accounts and passwords, the list of suppliers, an itemised current stock listing (estimated value of £4,000) and a twenty-page document I prepared, describing all the routine admin and maintenance tasks. We sit opposite each other, and their paperwork spills out on to the table, legal documents with embossed emblems, more forms for signature and a printout of next month's rota, with names barely legible due to the minuscule font size. Iris is holding her notepad and pen.

"Can we talk about the staffing for the next few weeks?" says Tom.

"Sure, we normally do the rota four weeks in advance. People need to know when they are scheduled." I point to their printout. "I've not had a chance to update it, so Kieran is still showing, but he won't be here obviously."

"We've been thinking about that, and we would like Kieran to stay on. We'll need someone to manage when we're not here. Is that okay?" says Tom.

"You'll need to ask Kieran. He was planning on dropping in tomorrow morning to make sure you can all the systems are working. Then I know he has an interview in Leamington on Tuesday."

"Okay, we'll talk to him in the morning," he says.

Iris opens her notebook; it looks like she has a list of questions. "How do we log into the CCTV system, so we can see the cameras on our phones?"

I point to my one-page document, with the heading, 'Accounts and Passwords.' "First you need to download the app, then use these login details and this I.P. address. Let's do that now," I say.

Louise, Nia, Grace and Priya appear at the top of the stairs.

"We've finished the cleaning now," Louise calls out. "The only thing left is to cash up the till. We just wanted to come up and say goodbye."

I jump up from my chair and walk towards them. "Thank you so much. I'm going to miss you guys," I say.

"We can't wait to read your book," says Priya.

"Are we going to be in it?" asks Nia.

"I haven't started yet. Would you like to be in it?" I say.

"I quite like the idea of being in a book," says Grace.

"Me too," say Nia and Priya together.

"Noted," I say.

I give Louise a hug and high-five Grace, Nia and Priya – I'm not sure a hug would have been appropriate. "Thank you and au revoir," I say.

I spend another hour or so with Tom and Iris, going through all their questions and walking them through the handover manual. We then cash up the till together. My emotional state is a concurrence of relief and sadness in the knowledge that I am about to close up for the last time. I do a final check of the kitchen, set the alarm, turn off the lights, exit the shop and lock the front door. I hand over the keys and we shake hands. I walk away.

REFLECTIONS

O ur journey started with an opportunity: savings in the bank, the freedom to work from home and a full tank of unbridled enthusiasm. We entered the coffee shop industry as rookies, attempting to carve out a quality niche in a market dominated by big consumer brands.

The first three months were about finding our feet and trying to establish our identity, but our initial excitement gave way to despondency when I produced our first profit and loss report. The clarity of the problem hit me like a slap in the face. Despite having a great customer following, this much-loved coffee shop was loss-making and on a trajectory to insolvency. The staffing costs were too high, our working procedures inefficient and we couldn't cope with surge demand. It was as if we had affixed a pair of skis to our feet for the first time and launched ourselves straight into a high-adrenaline black run. We would attempt to glide down the slope, whilst still learning how to swerve, and in full awareness that we may not reach the end without any broken bones. A more cautious beginner would have started on the green run and steadily progressed to the level of demonstrable competence.

Yet, our original intention was for a modest start-up operation, and we restricted our search to rental units costing no more than

£10,000 a year, with seating for up to thirty people. The Steam Station would have been the perfect start-up operation. However, pulling out of that deal was the correct decision as there would have been little chance of building any feasible customer base due to such little footfall. Our impatience and over-confidence led to our folly of acquiring a business we were ill-equipped to manage.

Our Achilles heel was food production, and this was the area that needed someone with strong hospitality management experience. The problem was simple enough to understand: our prepare-to-order food operation was time consuming and resource intensive. Switching to pre-packaged, ready-to-heat products would have resolved the speed of service issue, but that would compromise quality, and make us no different to the common-or-garden chain coffee shop. Kieran and the management staff were able to make some improvements, such as adding higher priced food items to the menu, but this was like bailing water out of a sinking ship using a twelve-ounce cappuccino cup. We weren't addressing the root cause. I did consider the option of recruiting a general hospitality manager – someone who could do all aspects of management and sort out food service, but to get that level of experience would add in the region of £2,700 to the monthly payroll bill. Perhaps that would have been an investment worth making.

My strategy for edging the business towards profitability was for me to help more in the shop, such as doing Saturday and Sunday shifts. Sharon once said, "You're an idiot for working like this." (She meant it in a caring way). But, in the moment, I felt there was no other way out and I was still clinging to the prospect of profitability. On reflection, my strategy was neither sensible nor sustainable.

Ultimately, it was the timing of the hospitality curveballs that bought us to our knees, specifically the 'danger to health' heat-wave, the repeated price rises from suppliers and kitchen closures due to staff absence. All of this occurred against the backdrop of a 'cost-of-living-crisis,' which made consumers more price sensitive. Attributing this to bad luck would be a cop-out. A good leader anticipates dangers and opportunities and adapts accordingly – a bit like an airline pilot changing their flight-plan when alerted to upcoming turbulence.

As for missed opportunities, there were community events which doubled the footfall on our doorstep. If we had prepared for such events, we could have doubled our takings-at-the-till for those days.

A coffee shop of this scale needs an experienced leader, who is hospitality-minded and business-focussed. I was unable to provide that leadership due to my lack of hospitality experience and the fact I had a fulltime commitment to another job. One may argue that a good leader does not need to have a background in the industry to be effective and he/she just needs to assemble a competent team, but I feel this is a bit like a football club appointing a tennis coach as their manager. Success in one discipline does not transfer to another, not least because there would be little credibility in the eyes of the team doing the work. I recall one day when one of the grinders jammed, I called Jon (the previous owner), who came in to show me how to unjam it and clean it. The staff were so happy to see him, and they all had a chat with him. He built the business from the ground up and knew how everything worked in the shop and was always available to resolve issues. The staff had confidence in his leadership and that gave them emotional security. For many of the existing staff, his leaving left a void that I was never going to be able to fill.

Tensions between myself and the staff arose as some staff members felt I was creating a stressful work environment. Kieran became the buffer between the staff and me – he had empathy for staff who felt overworked, but still recognised the need for better financial performance. Of course, in the absence of radical changes to ways of working, this was an impossible balancing act. Despite these moments of disagreement, we did enjoy some fun times and good camaraderie. I empowered the managers to organise the staff and make the day-to-day decisions. The staff supported each other and, like a well-practised sports team, each knew when to jump in and help where needed. Best of all was the staff-customer dynamic. I've never come across anywhere else where the staff collectively receive Christmas cards from the customers, all of them saying something along the lines of, "to all the wonderful staff at Arden's."

The one thing I am proud of, and the thing I miss most of all, is the social rhythm of Arden's. The regularity of the daily hubbub, the early morning club, the school dads and their kids. To many, this is more than a refuelling stop; it feels as though Arden's is part of the town's social infrastructure, serving the needs of those who would otherwise have a deficit of social connection. Then there is the banter. I recall handing over the wrong coffee order once. "They'll employ anyone here nowadays," was the customer's reaction, delivered with a smile and received with good humour, as intended. The artists' community, the children's workshops, the mothers' groups, the Zumba ladies, the families and their dogs, and all those regulars who come here because "'the staff are so nice.'" This place has given me a whole new perspective on the benefits of casual social interactions.

A dilemma I continuously struggled with was how to compensate staff fairly, whilst still making a profit. Staffing is the greatest cost in this business. When I took on the coffee shop, the statutory minimum wage for people of age twenty-three and over was just under £9.00 an hour and a little over £6.50 an hour for an eighteen-year-old. This increases in April of each year, and from April 2024, is £11.44 an hour for a twenty-one-year-old. We had a tip jar on the counter, and tips would be shared out proportionately depending on total hours worked over a monthly period. Someone who had worked full-time hours would receive in the region of £30 for the month! All things considered, this is a paltry reward for a physically tiring job, which includes unsociable weekend working.

The challenge for the coffee shop owner is to balance equitable compensation against reasonable prices. Factor in the above-inflation price increases of electricity and food staples, and the £3 cappuccino is a thing of the past. Most customers understand such cost pressures. In fact, I don't recall a shop customer complaining about my prices. The impact, as I see it, is that some customers may now think twice about buying that second cup of coffee in a day. Nevertheless, coffee shops are here to stay, not least because they provide a much-valued social experience. Therefore, the dilemma of equitable compensation versus reasonable prices will always remain a hospitality challenge.

The indulgence of coffee shop ownership comes with a personal cost. Prior to embarking on this journey, the hours from 5 a.m. until 8 a.m. were reserved for my exercise, meditation and self-learning. This routine was displaced by business administration, such as paying invoices, calculating payroll, reviewing job candidates and bookkeeping. Then there were the weekends working in the shop. This combination of mentally and physically demanding work, in addition to my regular job, is a lifestyle that became unrewarding and punishing. It was as if I was taking part in a long-distance run with no finishing line and no finisher's medal. In the end, it was the culmination of coffee-shop stresses, hospitality curveballs and an increasing burden from my day job that caused me to reassess my lifestyle choice. I walked into this business in full awareness that I would be a part-time leader, learning on the job, but I naively assumed that a well-oiled machine like this would operate with minimal management guidance. After all, how difficult can it be to run a coffee shop?

The one thing I feel I did do well (eventually) was the financials – bookkeeping, payroll, business performance monitoring. I never missed a bill payment, and only once did I make an error on payroll – a minor one for a small group of people – which I corrected on the same day. My financial monitoring routine allowed me to forecast cash flows and gain visibility of an impending cliff-edge, i.e., the point of insolvency, and this was my greatest fear. Selling the business was my way of failing gracefully; it allowed me to retire from this perpetual race without harm, whilst also avoiding a forced closure situation, which would have left the staff out of work at a moment's notice.

Do other independent coffee shop owners suffer the same as I do? Is a question I often asked myself. So I prepared a short survey and circulated it to other independent operators. I managed to get twenty responses. When asked about the biggest cost overhead, 78% of responders said it was staffing. However, when asked about what proportion of net revenue is consumed by staff costs, 66% of them reported this to be below that magical 40% threshold. I discovered that 34% of responders were not yet making a profit and another 34% had to wait over one year to become profitable. For most, this was their first and only coffee shop, confirming my assumption that to become successful, one needs to learn by doing and allow for a period of business losses. The most interesting response was to a question on the work/life balance of the coffee shop owner. 30% reported that they were 'stressed and exhausted.' The largest proportion responded to say they were 'working long hours but enjoy what they are doing.'

My conclusion from this (small-scale) survey is that personal stresses and business constraints are part and parcel of being an independent coffee shop owner. I had an even bigger problem as I was simultaneously trying to do another full-time job.

On my last day, after I returned home, I made one of my infrequent Facebook posts, announcing my exit from this venture. I was humbled by the many comments from friends, such as:

"You are awesome for trying something new, be proud!" (Zoe)

"You tried! Also, for what it's worth, you have a great personality for a coffee shop, so maybe someday!"

"Every entrepreneur has a list of 'failures' that they learned from. Think it was Wayne Gretzky who said, '100% of the shots I didn't take I don't score!' When you are ready to go again, you will almost certainly be surprised by what you might achieve. And

even if you decide not to go again, you took a shot that most people never do, so credit to you."

Christmas time of 2022 was relatively restful – I think of it as my decompression period, although I sometimes jolted myself awake at night because I was dreaming of being back in the coffee shop facing up to another calamity such as a closed kitchen or being unable to pay the rent or run payroll.

Would I do this again?
I am often tempted. Let's see.

End

Printed in Great Britain
by Amazon

42705577R00148